Fraser Sandeman

Angling Travels in Norway

Vol. 3

Fraser Sandeman

Angling Travels in Norway
Vol. 3

ISBN/EAN: 9783337212865

Printed in Europe, USA, Canada, Australia, Japan

Cover: Foto ©Andreas Hilbeck / pixelio.de

More available books at **www.hansebooks.com**

Angling Travels
in Norway

BY

FRASER SANDEMAN,
AUTHOR OF
"BY HOOK AND BY CROOK," ETC.

ILLUSTRATED
BY PENCIL, BRUSH, AND CAMERA,
AND
COLOURED PLATES OF SALMON FLIES BY THE AUTHOR;
ALSO A
PLATE OF FAVOURITE FLIES FOR NORWAY.

LONDON: CHAPMAN & HALL, LD.
1895.

PREFACE.

THE purpose of the following pages is to describe some few districts, rivers, lakes, and fish of Norway with which I am acquainted, and to indicate in what respects they differ with those of the British Isles from an angler's point of view. I have ventured to give some hints upon the various methods of angling and its requirements, also upon the treatment of fish alive and dead, which I trust may be of interest and service to naturalists and sportsmen.

In writing of a country, it is difficult to omit mention of her people, although one might prefer to avoid so delicate a subject.

"I like the people," is a phrase frequently uttered by visitors to Norway, and probably expresses correctly enough the British opinion of our Scandinavian neighbours; but it is rather a large order for individual foreigners to declare that they like or dislike a whole nation, so I have merely stated how I have been treated by dwellers in town and country, including those who are accustomed to have dealings with sportsmen and travellers, and others inhabiting more remote districts, where visitors are scarce and no fixed rules or tariffs exist.

The chapters in which are related the details of various expeditions in quest of fish are intended to afford some idea of what the angler may expect as regards sport, and to describe Norwegian life in hotel, private house, farm, and camp. In giving the names of the rivers and districts in which some of my experiences have been gained, I have adopted the suggestion of kindly critics of "By Hook and by Crook," and I take this opportunity to thank them and my readers for their gracious reception of that work. Although the technical illustrations are roughly drawn, I trust they may serve their purpose, and, with the more artistic process productions from photographs, convey faithful impressions of sport in a sporting country.

FRASER SANDEMAN.

ARMATHWAITE, *May*, 1895.

CONTENTS.

PART I.

CHAPTER		PAGE
I.	INTRODUCTORY	1
II.	DANGER AHEAD	6
III.	THE YEAR IN NORWAY	10
IV.	CLIMATE AND WEATHER	16
V.	RIVERS	21
VI.	NETS AND TRAPS IN THE FJORDS AND RIVERS	28
VII.	THE LAKES OF NORWAY	39
VIII.	THE COUNTRY-FOLK	43
IX.	BOATS	50
X.	SALMONIDÆ OF NORWAY	54
XI.	TO DISTINGUISH BETWEEN TROUT AND SMOLT	102
XII.	TACKLE FOR NORWAY	106
XIII.	HARLING AND BOAT-ANGLING	114
XIV.	UPON RENTING AND LETTING SALMON RIVERS	127
XV.	PRAWN-FISHING FOR SALMON	137
XVI.	TO SPLIT, CURE, AND SMOKE SALMON	143

PART II.

NORWEGIAN SKETCHES.

CHAPTER		PAGE
XVII.	SÖRENDAL ...	148
XVIII.	VADSÆTH AND SVARDAL ...	173
XIX.	VOSS AND THE EVANGER RIVER	199
XX.	NORDLAND ...	236
	APPENDIX	281

LIST OF ILLUSTRATIONS.

	PAGE
SAGHOUG POOL ...	*Frontispiece*
FJORD-NET ...	32
SALMON-TRAP ...	36
A RIVER SALMON-TRAP ...	37
A NORWEGIAN FAMILY PARTY ...	44
THREE LITTLE MAIDS FROM SCHOOL ...	49
SALMON, HEAD OF	56
TABLE OF SALMONIDÆ	*Between* 56 *and* 57
SALMON, GILL-COVERS	58
,, JAWS AND TONGUE ...	59
,, THORAX ...	60
SEA-TROUT, HEAD OF	83
,, TAIL, GILL-COVER, TONGUE, AND JAWS ...	84
,, MALFORMED HEAD	86
HERLING, GILL-COVER AND TAIL ...	88
BULL-TROUT, HEAD OF ...	89
,, GILL-COVERS	90
,, ,, ,, ...	91
,, JAWS, TONGUE, AND TAILS ...	93
TROUT, HEAD OF	95
,, JAWS, TONGUE, AND GILL-COVER ...	96
CHAR, TAIL OF	100
FAVOURITE FLIES FOR NORWAY ...	*To face* 106
OLE AND I ...	108
ALL SIXES AND SEVENS	113
FIVE MINUTES' REST	119
PRAWN-TACKLE	140
,,	141
TO SPLIT A FISH	143
,, ,,	144
,, ,,	146

List of Illustrations.

	PAGE
CHRISTIANSUND ...	151
EIKEFJORD, 7 A.M. ...	179
VADSÆTH LAKE ...	183
„ „ OUTLET OF ...	184
VADSÆTH RIVER ...	188
HEAD OF VADSÆTH LAKE ...	190
SVARDAL FJELDS ...	191
HOPEN	196
VOSSEVANGEN LAKE ...	202
LILAND'S HOTEL, BÜLKEN ...	203
THE VOSS NATIONAL COSTUME ...	205
A SALMON-TRAP	208
THE FOSS	210
VIEW OF RAPID FROM SUSPENSION BRIDGE	213
THE STAGE AT SAGHOUG ...	216
SAGHOUG POOL	219
TWO HOURS' SPORT IN SAGHOUG	223
RIVER AT HEAD OF VOSSEVANGEN LAKE	227
FOSS AT VOSSEVANGEN	230
SALTEN FJORD ...	242
A LADY OF LOFOTEN ...	243
A NORSK "HERRING-SMACK"	246
ROGNAN	250
MAP OF SALTEN RIVER	253
GRILSE, SEA-TROUT, ETC.	255
THE FORSTASSISTENT'S HOUSE	260
JUNKERDAL	269

COLOURED ILLUSTRATIONS.

1. LLANOVER	... To face	106
2. BRANSTY ...	„	109
3. SAGHOUG	„	110
4. GÜLA ...	„	112

[*As reference is made in the following pages to fishing-tackle, etc., it is but fair to the proprietors or makers of such to say that the Author has no pecuniary interest in any fishing-tackle or fishing-gear.*]

ANGLING TRAVELS IN NORWAY.

PART I.

CHAPTER I.

INTRODUCTORY.

CHANGE of scene is not infrequently prescribed by the physician; and who shall say that novelty has not a charm for those of robust health?

Most of us can recall to mind some first visit to a particular spot where commonplace incidents felicitously combined to fill our cup of enjoyment to overflowing, leaving behind them impressions which memory has delighted to keep quick.

Indeed, so delightful have been those recollections that we have been prompted to repeat our visit—alas! only to meet with disappointment.

Why the disappointment? The component parts of that previous good time were again present, and we were prepared to take our part with the fullest intention to continue exactly where we had left off, but somehow or another an indescribable *something* appeared to be lacking, and the function had not the " go " of heretofore.

Others enjoyed themselves as we had done, but for us the novelty had departed, its interest was shallow, and its mysteries easy of penetration. Year by year we reap similar disappointments in the various walks and studies of life, which afford part material for the erection of that structure named " experience."

Without a fair stock of knowledge of the world and its inmates, we approach each new situation with diffidence, for we have little confidence in our behaviour under novel circumstances, but later, when the apprenticeship of years has been intelligently served—we meet each new task with a bold front, conscious of resource, and as advancement is made towards perfection we even thirst for opportunities to afford exercise of our skill.

"Familiarity breeds contempt"—so in no pursuit should self-reliance, the fruit of experience, be permitted to engender relaxation of vigilance and observation, or the proverb, "A little knowledge is a dangerous thing," may be found too true. Such confidence might indeed be termed the abuse of lessons of the past, which should be utilized more economically to assimilate present situations with others previously encountered, thus providing a method of procedure conducive to ultimate success.

Introductory. 3

In short, we should not expose ourselves to the risks of overweening confidence, whether in the pursuit of profession, business, or sport.

Of intellectual pursuits, pastimes, field-sports, or what you will, those may be said to have asserted supremacy which have best stood the test of time. Upon examination, such will reveal the possession of infinite variety in detail, an expansive field for study, and stimulant for research.

These are the legacies bequeathed to the sportsman—I mean the *sportsman* in a true sense, the man who studies the natural history of his quarry—not the man who pulls the trigger at a bundle of feathers whose contents are to him of little interest, nor him who employs the speed of horse or dog simply as an instrument for gambling. A spectator of a glove-fight, the backer of a dog or horse who has no interest in the animal beyond his bet, is, in our days, flattered by a portion of the Press into the belief that he is a *sportsman;* but in my humble opinion it would be preferable, in order to avoid confusion, to grant to him who pursues the sports of the field the exclusive right to his own title, and to describe gamblers and bettors by a more appropriate term.

Of the many branches of " sport," none has better stood the test of time than angling—none has more votaries ; and although, as in other studies, we commence where our fathers concluded, there remains a vast amount to be learnt both in the art itself and in the habits of the game.

Our methods of angling are no doubt much improved, and in fish culture and ichthyology we have made considerable strides, but towards the elucidation of the incidents of some stages in the life of the Salmonidæ we are so distant that we yet appear to be nearer the beginning than the end.

The observation of fish while angling in foreign waters affords the opportunity to compare their habits with those of dwellers in the lakes and rivers of our own country, and for this purpose visits to Norway are of rare interest to the angler-naturalist.

He will probably make no startling discovery, it is true, but he will ascertain the peculiarities of the waters of the country, the requirements for angling, and the habits of fish under circumstances which do not exist elsewhere, and turning homewards with his harvest garnered, he will acknowledge to himself that had it been reaped ere he first had put foot in the country he would have commenced at the point where he concluded—to his advantage as regards sport.

Such was my impression at the termination of my first visit to Scandinavia, as, with my kind host, I made the sad return passage by river to the fjord; and to enable anglers, no farther advanced than I, to take up the thread

Introductory. 5

where it snapped with me is the object of the following chapters.

The first portion of this volume is principally devoted to the more technical matters relating to ichthyology and angling in Norway, which I am afraid are somewhat dry reading, and in the second portion I have endeavoured to place before my readers descriptions of a few angling trips, with the hope that they may convey some little idea of the difficulties and the requirements of Norwegian angling.

CHAPTER II.

DANGER AHEAD.

THE natural habits of the various species of Salmonidæ, when uncontrolled, are identical all Europe over; each would behave in precisely the same manner whether existing in Great Britain, Portugal, or Norway; they are to the manner born, and incapable of aping the conduct of other species.

This trait is common to all kinds of animals, so the angler should approach a strange sphere of operations with a firm conviction that he will meet his own familiar friends, and he should not permit unaccustomed surroundings to influence him in this respect.

Climatic influence, conformation of the watershed, and the nature of the river-bed, impart to fisheries individual peculiarity, and the combination of these factors produces a result suitable or inimical to the existence of fish.

When fish occupy haunts embracing the necessities or even luxuries of existence, they are loath to quit, notwithstanding that changes effected by various causes may have rendered the tenancy less *enjoyable;* they, so to say, put up with the inconvenience, and, as long as they are able, make the best of a bad job, but, when free agents, will rather forsake such homes than alter their *natural habits* to meet the exigencies of the situation.

In short, rivers and lakes may alter, but, unless compelled, fish will not.

Angling in Norway is conducted by the methods practised in our home waters, but the nature of the country and climate demands alterations in detail; therefore it is essential that the angler should appreciate the conditions which afford a key to the situation.

He starts with one certainty, however, in that he is about to fish a strange river in a strange country—an awkward combination—so he must call experience to his aid, and endeavour to diagnose the pools without loss of time; with this object, he should keep his eyes open, and concentrate attention while noting the size of the river and the formation of its bed, banks, and pools.

The possession of a good eye for the lie of fish is a gift granted to the few who have made a study of natural history at the waterside, and these become so conversant with their subject that they for the time being seem as if merged into it; but some seem never to acquire this sympathy, however much they may fish.

Most of the Norwegian salmon rivers worth fishing are

rented by natives of the British Isles, by Norsk anglers, or by speculators; and one or two in the extreme north, such as the Tana, can be fished upon payment of the Norwegian and Russian licences. Trustworthy information as to the average yearly take upon each river can only be obtained from one who has fished it recently; any other source is more or less unreliable.

Norway has her late and early rivers, and many of the best for angling purposes are of such width that "harling" is the only practical method by which they can be fished; others, or beats of others, hardly admit the use of aught but the fly. Again, upon some, the fish, when caught, become the property of the riparian proprietors; so the angler intending to take a fishing had better first determine what he wants, and then endeavour to get it.

The salmon-fishing season commences towards the end of May upon early rivers, and about the end of June upon the later ones, and it may be taken as a general rule that the first four to six weeks are the best upon most rivers; but there are a few which fish best towards the end of July until the close of the season—*i.e.* September 15, —except in a few instances where extensions have been granted.

Fortunate is the man who can await at his riverside the ascent of the fish, and see the season out; but as, for private reasons, many "go out" at intermediate dates, I propose to briefly sketch the events of an average year upon a Norwegian river, in order that the angler may form some idea of what has taken place prior to his arrival, and what may be expected to occur later.

CHAPTER III.

THE YEAR IN NORWAY.

In order to obtain a sharply defined point in the yearly existence of the salmon, we will fix upon September 15 (the commencement of the ordinary close-time) as the date of our departure.

The summer is well-nigh past, the nights are drawing in, the annual snow upon the mountain and hill summits has supplied food for the rivers, or partly remains with the glacier ice to defy the rays of the feeble autumn sun.

Thus the rivers are mostly dependent upon springs for supply, and, in consequence, are at about their lowest level until the advent of frost.

The pools are now stocked with fish deep in colour and far advanced towards spawning condition, those in the upper stretches having selected favourite sites ere this, while later arrivals have gradually appropriated the lower berths, all awaiting a fitting time and season. The spawning operations now commence, and will continue into the winter season, which may set in at any date after the beginning of November; then many of the rivers become clothed in ice to such depth that while in this state they are used as roads.

From now until the break up of frost in the following spring the inhabitants of such rivers and lakes are prisoners, merely refreshed by the under-current provided by springs.

The temperature during the next few months compels the fatness of the clouds to fall as snow, and preserves it as such throughout the winter.

A copious supply of snow before Christmas is anxiously awaited by those interested in angling, and, to ensure a good season, this should be augmented by other falls during the early months of the following year.

The snow falling in December becomes hard and compact by the frost of the next few months, and is further compressed by subsequent falls, the total forming solid material capable of stubborn resistance to the rays of the next summer's sun, thus providing the angler with a lengthy season.

If the snow stored up on mountains and fjelds shall but have fallen during the later months of winter, the coming angling season will probably be of short duration, for the supply is soft, and easy of disintegration by rain and sun.

With successive snowfalls as above described, the angling prospects are of good promise, yet they are by no means assured; various courses of events, as regards weather and temperature, may easily occur to mar the brightest hopes.

In one case, continued rainfall may melt the supply of snow *en bloc*, flooding the rivers, and then leaving them at summer level, with little chance of improvement for that season. On the other hand, the temperature during the summer months may be so low that much snow remains unmelted, and the rivers, thus deprived of supplies, soon fall in. Or, in a third case, long-continued hot summer weather may melt the snow, and bring about one continued flood, and then leave the river entirely dependent upon rain for further supply. These are the conditions which militate against the fulfilment of initiatory promise, and complications of them may easily arise.

With the advent of warmer temperature, the thick coatings of ice, which for so long a period have clothed the rivers and watersheds, will commence to give and break up, and pile one upon another as the stream impels them to the fjords.

The huge masses grind and crash against the banks and other obstructions, giving signal to the country-folk to witness the annual spectacle.

By the middle of May, this country, which for so

many months has been hushed in the deathlike sleep of winter, commences to open out—the hillsides, which until recently were white, now stream with water, the valleys awaken, and vegetation springs to life.

The pine, the juniper, and silver-birch put forth new shoots, and the grass becomes of emerald green. Norway is at last awake, and her valleys and rivers free themselves of flood water and *débris* of winter, putting their homes in order for the reception of their annual visitors—the fish of the sea and the fowls of the air. The divers, ducks, martins, swallows, and small migrants appear as if by magic, seeming impatient for the leafy growth which will afford cover for their domestic arrangements. The bears, with appetites whetted by hibernation, will drop down from the fjelds to indulge in sheep-stealing, and anglers arrive in pursuit of fish.

Towards the early days of June, many of the rivers will have become free from flood-water, and gradually fine down to a condition favourable to the ascent of fish, which are waiting at the entrance of the fjords, or the mouths of the rivers, until their waters shall be raised to a suitable temperature.

Fish are now being caught in the nets at the river mouth and all along the fjord, but none are found in the river itself, so there can be no doubt that temperature controls their movements. The natives prophesy that with a week of warm weather they may be expected, and subsequent events prove them to be correct.

A week of inactivity is no pleasant prospect for the angler, but in consideration of the volume of icy water pouring into the fjord it is but reasonable that the rise in temperature is so long delayed, in spite of tidal influence.

Cold northerly winds, attended by sleet and rain, will naturally delay ascent of fish, and the angler may possibly have to bide his time until the middle of June with the only consolation—better too soon than too late.

Upon early rivers, even in a late season, the middle of June should herald a run of fish, then work begins, and the angler must settle to business, fishing, according to his lights, until the middle of August, when small waters and golden-tinted flanks will warn him that it be time to desist.

The lakes of Norway are often frozen during the winter months, and naturally take long to thaw, when they have no stream to sweep away their ice cover, and the fjelds by which they are approachable are so wet and rotten that they are almost impracticable until July; but this delay is of little importance to the angler, as the inhabitants of the lakes do not regain fair condition until the middle of that month, or even the early days of August.

The Year in Norway.

In this manner, for some months after spawning, the lake-fish are dependent for nourishment upon bottom feeding, consequently their convalescence is greatly retarded.

I have in this chapter endeavoured to convey to the reader some idea of the events of a year in Norway, and will proceed with a few details as to the climate and temperature that may be experienced during the angling season.

CHAPTER IV.

CLIMATE AND WEATHER.

It is impossible to accurately forecast the meteorological conditions of a Norwegian summer, for the clerk of the weather makes arrangements with the same disregard for the interests of anglers and agriculturists as he displays in other parts of the world; his sway is undeniable and his reign supreme.

It is no use to kick against the pricks, no use to grumble, and of no use to speculate how more pleasant the time might be if we could arrange the order of events more to our liking.

The only practical system is that which provides against all contingencies, and renders the helpless mortal fit to face the foe.

In the ordinary course of events, the Norwegian summer, with broiling sun and cloudless sky, will take the field ere the middle of June, and will more or less hold the boards until the end of August, but there are exceptions, and these exceptions must be provided against.

It may easily happen that north-westerly winds, accompanied by sleet and rain, will rule the roast, and refuse to be ousted for a month or two.

The sun may assert his power now and again, and upon each occasion summer appears to have arrived; but without warning the wind shifts back to the old quarter, and the murky clouds retrace their steps.

In the morning I have set out under a brilliant sun and cloudless sky, anticipating a hot day, and my hopes were realized until perhaps about three p.m., when suddenly the wind has backed, and I have been treated to an icy draught from the snow-clad mountains, and have turned up my coat-collar and shivered.

The system of clothing adopted by the natives of any particular portion of the earth's surface is always indicative of the climate's nature and vagaries, and the visitor in Norway cannot fail to remark what care the natives take of their chests and throats. They frequently wear what may be named a chest-protector—a kind of thick pad which commences under the waistcoat, and reaches nearly to the chin; they also show partiality for a woollen scarf around the neck, which a deal of hot sun will fail to remove, and yet they will wade in icy water, and be wet all day, without anxiety as to health. The reason of these precautions is not far to seek, for the valleys are deep cuttings, and create a draught either up or down, which must be kept at bay.

To successfully cope with these peculiarities of climate, the angler should be provided with suits of clothing such as he would wear during winter, spring, and summer in the British Isles, not forgetting wading trousers, wading stockings, and mackintosh coat down to his heels, and if he include a Shetland jersey he probably will not lament.

The reader must not understand that any particular weather is general throughout Norway during any one season, and he must note that conditions which are favourable to some districts may preclude chance of sport in others, and in this direction it is apparent that a supply of water which floods a small river may barely suffice to maintain a larger one in angling trim for a considerable time.

Cold winds much retard the snow in melting, and maintain the water of the fjords and rivers at a low temperature, and under such circumstances the angling season will be late in starting.

Upon the other hand, warm weather, attended by rain, will quickly melt and disintegrate the snow upon the highlands; and, if this state of affairs should continue, the season will be short, and may even terminate almost before it has commenced.

Climate and Weather.

As a general rule, the prospects of an angling season upon rivers not supplied by glaciers can be pretty accurately gauged by the stock of snow up country; but, as above indicated, such calculations may easily be upset. It stands to reason that the smaller rivers and the upper stretches of large ones will be well served by a wet season which possibly may render the bigger waters useless on account of continued floods, and then there is the reverse side of the picture, viz. a cold dry season with little snow upon the hills and mountains, consequently no water in the small rivers, and only sufficient in the larger to afford a couple of weeks' sport.

The conditions requisite to constitute an ideal season from the angler's point of view would be somewhat upon these lines—plenty of snow before and after Christmas, warm weather during end of May and June, with occasional cool and cloudy days, then, with occasional rain in July, the rivers should fish well for a couple of months, and it is indeed fortunate if spates should occur during the weekly close-time for netting in the fjords, to which I shall have occasion to refer later on.

The man who can spend the months of June, July, and August in Norway is fortunate, as he reaps the season's harvest; but he who is obliged to fix his visit to extend over a shorter period may easily miss the mark in this as in other countries.

It is difficult to ascertain the season's prospects before going out; indeed, the "old hands" who annually visit the country appear to take little or no pains to obtain information, for the simple reason that they intend to go out early and see the season through; but, in any case, not much could be ascertained beyond the quantity of snow up country.

The angler with but a limited time at his disposal must put all his eggs in one basket, for the distance is too great to permit of leaving the country for a while, to return when the water is in order; thus, under adverse circumstances, a deal of time may be spent unprofitably, which, if nearer home, the angler could utilize for other purposes, and place to his credit, to be drawn upon later.

If I were free to select a month's salmon fishing, I should, upon the early rivers, take from June 15 to July 15, and for sea-trout and lake fishing would prefer from July 15 to August 15.

With axioms as described above, it is scarcely possible that a season with bad prospects can prove a good one, while promises, like pie-crust, are made but to be broken, and the fairest hopes may never be realized.

CHAPTER V.

RIVERS.

THE ways and means by which Norwegian rivers obtain their supplies have such variety that it is but natural that the inland fisheries of the country should differ to a considerable extent with one another, and to a yet greater degree as compared with those of a less unconventional country such as Great Britain.

In this and other chapters, be it understood, I summon the aid of comparison, not for purpose of disparagement or praise, but in the endeavour to enable the reader, by the assistance of a familiar scene, to realize a country of which he is personally ignorant.

Norway contains rivers of all sizes, some glacier-fed, some snow-fed, and others with watersheds of such little altitude that after the first break-up of winter they are entirely dependent upon rainfall for supply.

The largest, such as the Tana and Namsen, are *bigger* than any river in the British Isles; the medium-size rivers would compare with the Tay, Tweed, or Solway rivers; while the smaller ones are about on a par, as regards volume, with the Helmsdale, North Esk, etc., and then come the really small streams which may be compared with the sea-trout rivers of Wales and the west of Scotland; thus it is essential that the angler should be acquainted with the size of his river before he " goes out," in order that his tackle be suitable for the task in hand.

In an ordinary summer, the heat of the sun's rays will day by day melt sufficient quantities of snow and ice to maintain the snow- and glacier-fed rivers in angling trim until the end of July, or even later, and the supply from these sources naturally depends upon the temperature of the day and night.

The produce of the day's sun will make itself apparent towards evening, causing the river to rise a few inches or several feet; then, as the night passes away, the water will again fall in until upon the following morning it will be slightly below the level of that previous. But if perchance the nights should be hot, the snow may continue to melt throughout the four-and-twenty hours, and the river in consequence be in a continual state of flood, and thus the reserve of snow is not so economically used in the angler's interests as if the nights were sufficiently cool to check it in melting.

Towards the end of the season, as the stock of snow

Rivers.

becomes reduced, this evening rise of water is of short duration, and the river may be again fishable within a few hours, until when the annual snow has become exhausted, or the daily temperature is too low to melt that which may remain, then the river becomes dead-low.

The angler who has learnt to regard snow broth as his *bête noir* is apt to be startled by the statement that it is upon plentiful supplies of snow that his sport to a great extent depends, and it is excusable if with some slight trepidation he approach such fields and pastures new.

But there is no need of alarm, for the snow-water has no resemblance to the same mess in Great Britain, for in its descent from the hills and mountains it gets so tossed about that it becomes aërated and similar to the water in the rivers themselves.

During the first few weeks of the melting winter-snow, the hillsides are streaming with water in all directions; in fact, the country is nothing more nor less than an immense shower-bath, and as the streams issuing from glaciers and snow-fields speed on, to give their contribution to the rivers below, they are frequently precipitated from considerable heights, thus forming the waterfalls, or "fosses," which add so much to the scenic beauty of the country, and attract visitors from near and far.

The glacier-fed rivers being partially independent of

snow and rain for their supplies, afford the angler a greater certainty of sport in summers of average temperature, but when the winter's snow has melted, there often comes a period when the green glacier-water puts the river completely out of trim for angling to a distance of many miles; thus a short river of this description may give disappointing results.

It will be gathered from the foregoing remarks that in an average season the volume of water in the rivers is maintained at a fair height for from six weeks to a couple of months, and during this period is not subject to such frequent extremes as is the case in rivers which are fed by rain alone.

The migratory Salmonidæ, as might be expected, are aware of the probable order of events, and during the early part of the season, in the snow-fed and glacier-fed rivers, do not ascend in large "runs," as is their habit in countries where the date of the next spate is a matter of comparative uncertainty, but are content to keep dribbling up day by day in small batches, when unimpeded by obstacles such as nets, etc.

This procedure is favourable to the angler, as thereby he is provided with a daily supply of fresh-run fish. The rivers, whose temperatures favour the early running of fish, are frequently well stocked upon the opening of the season, and fine sport is obtained for a few weeks, then the daily takes grow smaller by degrees, while the smallest rivers provide no more than a week's fishing.

In Norway, as elsewhere, fish often run quickly through the lower portions of the rivers, and, in a big water especially, they will halt little *en route*; so, to take full advantage of opportunities, the angler fishing such should be constantly at work, paying particular attention to business during the weekly close-time for nets in the fjords, and at those hours by which the fish will reach his fishery as they ascend with each high tide at the river's mouth.

The pools and beds of Norwegian rivers are of every variety and formation; some are of solid rock; others are formed of cobbles, angular blocks of rock, and coarse gravel; while another variety is of fine gravel, studded with stones of all shapes and sizes.

Those pools, which are floored and walled in by solid rock, naturally retain their conformation, and when once learnt are known for ever; but those whose beds are composed of loose stones and gravel may from year to year be swept clean of all obstructions at the break-up of each winter's ice; and, in consequence, their characters are subject to frequent alteration, and their values as salmon-pools are increased or diminished as the case may be.

In some instances the gravel silted up by the floods

and ice-floes of successive springs will cause the river to deviate from the path it has used for a number of years; thus a good pool may be rendered useless, while the new passage which takes its place will in all likelihood be too rapid, for some years at least, to suit the requirements of fish.

Loose stones or boulders resting upon gravel have as insecure foundation as the house that is built upon sand; thus pools become bare wastes, robbed of charms which, if they could remain, would offer infallible inducements for fish.

Fish hurry through these stretches, and seek more congenial quarters where they can find shelters against the stream.

Notwithstanding the small accommodation for rest extended by these gravelly pools, exhausted nature compels the fish to take an easy now and again, to recruit strength, but they will delay as little as possible in uncongenial quarters.

To remedy the lack of suitable resting-places for fish in the gravelly pools, the proprietors or lessees upon many rivers resort to artificial means, either by dropping in rocks or by building structures of timber and boulders, but when such devices are adopted, much discretion is needed, for a big salmon-river is an awkward thing to play with; and when, in the natural course of events,

Rivers.

it is not unusual for half an acre of bank to be washed away, it can readily be understood that landowners look with a jealous eye upon systems for the improvement of angling which may possibly deprive them of their property.

To prevent the encroachment of rivers upon land, and to insure the safety of the post-roads, long and steep embankments of stone have frequently to be made, and as these can only be constructed at great cost, it follows that any meddling with the beds or banks of rivers is, to say the least of it, a hazardous procedure.

The land adjacent to some of the pools of many Norwegian rivers lies flat and low, and long backwaters are not uncommon which rise and fall with the main stream. These backwaters are invaluable as nurseries for the young Salmonidæ, who can thus exist and grow fat in comparative safety.

Some few lessees or proprietors of Norwegian rivers have gone to much expense in blasting the waterways and in the construction of passes and ladders to provide passages by which the fish can ascend to upper waters; and by these means many rivers have been much improved, while to others small benefit would appear to have accrued.

CHAPTER VI.

NETS AND TRAPS IN THE FJORDS AND RIVERS.

THE stock of salmon existing at the present time in Norwegian rivers is generally considered to be much less than in years gone by, and the cause of the decrease is attributed to the greed of the netsmen along the coast and at the mouths and along the margins of the fjords; and when it is considered that these arms of the sea, many of them some thirty miles or more in length, through which fish must pass *en route* to the rivers, are furnished at every promontory with an elaborate system of netting, it is apparent how great must be the odds against a fish emerging scathless from the ordeal.

Fish, like blind men, steer by the margin of the road, and it is obvious that their path is more nearly defined at points where the land projects out into the fjord, round which they must turn, so these are the positions generally selected for the setting of nets.

It is unnecessary here to enter into full details of the

Nets and Traps in the Fjords and Rivers.

increase of salmon-netting, but I may mention that about thirty years ago there were only about three hundred nets along the coast, whereas at the present time the number exceeds six thousand.

Whatever proficiency Norwegians may have attained in the capture of cod and the more common sea-fish, until, within recent years they would not appear to have possessed much aptitude in the capture of salmon, and the progress they have made in the art is mainly due to the adoption of the various patterns of nets and the methods of using them as practised in Great Britain, and in consequence they hold their tutors in considerable esteem.

Even at the present time in the northern districts of Norway, the flesh of the salmon is valuable for food only in the neighbourhood of its capture, but lower down the coast improved means of transport and the system of re-icing the packages during transit have opened up the industry of salmon-netting, and as the natives have a particularly keen scent for £ s. d., they are not slow to adopt the best systems for the purpose.

Their coffers were filling with the proceeds of the golden eggs while they paid not the slightest regard for the goose that laid them, and, as was certain to be the case, the stock of salmon gradually but surely decreased until even the extinction of the species seemed possible in the not-far-distant future.

The yearly captures both by net and rod were growing "smaller by degrees and beautifully less," and the reason was patent to all, but no measures were adopted to avert the disaster until the energetic protests of visitors from the British Isles—lessees of rivers—so far impressed the native authorities that at length the weekly close-time for nets was lengthened by a day, and the size of the mesh was also increased.

The latter restriction, however, was not to come into force until three years after the law was passed, and although the delay was to be regretted, it was only fair to grant the fishermen a reasonable time to wear out their nets then in use.

The new law regulating the size of mesh was, however, more fortunate than that which increased the weekly close-time, for the latter, to the great disappointment of those who have the true interests of the rivers at heart, was cancelled within a year of its introduction for political purposes by the same Government which passed it.

The various forms of net are not removed bodily from the water, but in most instances have merely the guiding-arm shifted; in others, the entrance to the bag is shut while the guiding-arm remains in position. Again, some nets and traps have an exit at the extremity of the bag which is opened during close-time.

I have frequently landed grilse weighing exactly four

Nets and Traps in the Fjords and Rivers. 31

pounds each which have just contrived to run through the nets, having the scales stripped from their skins from a distance of two inches in front of the fore extremity of the dorsal fin to two inches behind it; so it may be taken that a fish of this weight is the largest that can squeeze through.

It can easily be understood that the close-time can be disregarded with impunity in districts which contain miles upon miles of lonely fjord, which are rarely traversed by others than those directly or indirectly interested in the transgression of the law, and so over vast districts the close-time existed, or even now exists, but in name.

The fishermen seem to agree not to inform against one another, and it is no uncommon event for the nets to remain fishing when by rights they should be off duty.

In several instances those detected in disobedience to the law have pleaded ignorance, and not infrequently have been granted such an extension of time in which to pay the fine imposed that the penalty was reduced to little less than a farce.

In course of time, however, sufficient prosecutions have been put in force to prove that the proprietors and lessees were in grim earnest, and no doubt the close-time is now more generally observed, notwithstanding that more convictions are obtained.

Many of the fjord and river watchers have far from a

pleasant time while engaged in their arduous duties, and I recollect one of them telling me that some netsmen had threatened to put his head into a saw-mill if he interfered with their poaching proclivities.

In the years 1884–1886, the average number of convictions was seventy-three, and the amount of the

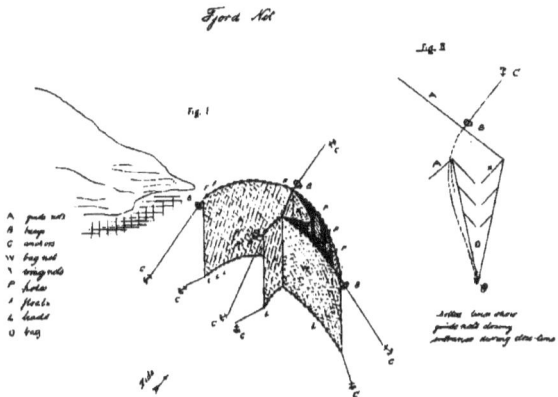

fines imposed was Kr. 1488; while during the years 1887–1891, the fines imposed annually amounted to Kr. 3390, divided amongst one hundred and sixty-three individuals.

Fixed walls of net guiding the fish into a pocket at the end are anchored along the edges of the fjords at each projecting angle of rock which the fish skirt in pursuit

Nets and Traps in the Fjords and Rivers. 33

of the river mouth; and, with the object of directing them to these points, fishermen frequently paint the rocks white in imitation of falling water, with intention to give fish the idea that a rivulet or beck runs in, and so to excite a curiosity that shall bring them into contact with the net.

This idea of whitening the rocks may have been original, but probably was suggested by the patches of white quartz which occasionally intersect the rocks at the water's edge, and to some extent appear to attract fish.

The angler has much to suffer in this sparsely inhabited country, yet he is spared some of the annoyances to be encountered upon the rivers of the United Kingdom—firstly, he is rarely troubled by kelts; and, secondly, there are few dead leaves to foul his hook; but in order that his life may not be one of unadulterated bliss, a few hazards are strewn in his path.

The consequences of a landslip in the course of a watershed or river may be fatal to angling for an entire season, on account of discoloration caused by the wash of marl or clay which keeps pouring in; then there is the annual transportation of pine logs down the rivers to the fjords, which frequently upsets all calculation, and, maybe for a day or two, renders a good water well-nigh unfishable.

I have frequently started casting from the boat in a state of water which almost guaranteed sport, and while in the act of casting have been thrown on my knees by the concussion caused by a pine log drifting down upon the boat, and, upon looking up-stream, to my dismay have viewed an endless string of these nuisances bearing down upon us.

Down they come along the stream side of your favourite pools, the ends alternately charging the banks and making a rare mess of the water, until first one and then another gets hitched up upon the banks or shallows as the water gradually falls in.

Towards the afternoon, most of the trunks will have passed by, or become hitched up, and you calculate upon a few hours of uninterrupted sport; but even in this you are disappointed, as the effect of the day's sun now causes the river to rise, and the anchored logs are again freed, to pursue their deadly course, and put an end to the day's angling.

You console yourself with the reflection that upon the morrow you will be unmolested, and betimes you set to work to make up for lost time, but here again you are out in your reckoning, for scarcely have you commenced fishing when a log comes bumping into the boat, a warning of more trouble.

The stream is more sparsely strewn with litter to-day than yesterday, as these are only the stragglers which have got hung up in banks and backwaters, and to get free

Nets and Traps in the Fjords and Rivers. 35

require the assistance of that gang of fiends in black who are now remorselessly wading all over the pool above, while freeing the pine logs with their twelve-foot hitchers.

You pull ashore to await their departure, and resolve to keep your temper, but, alas ! the gang requires food and rest, so they squat at the water's edge for an hour or two. It is no use your fishing above or below, for both have been disturbed alike, so you give it up until the evening. Later on you start afresh with yet a chance of sport, when in all probability the last two of the gang of woodmen will descend the river in a boat, in order to set afloat the most obstinate of the logs; thus the best part of two days' angling is completely ruined.

The operation of transporting logs could be performed during times of flood without hindrance to the angler, but this system would not suit the wily Norsk, for occasionally he might have to recover logs left high and dry some little distance inland, so he delays the descent of his property until later, usually selecting a period when the pools are in first-class angling trim.

A further cause of annoyance to anglers is found in the ubiquitous ferry-boat which is generally stationed opposite the best catch of the pool, and which, during the hay-making season, incessantly crosses and re-crosses the stream. In most countries, the ferry-boat is used with discretion upon salmon rivers, but the Norwegian is not by nature an angler, and it does not occur to him to extend to sportsmen any consideration in this direction.

The capture of migratory Salmonidæ in the rivers of Norway is regulated and controlled by laws distinct from those which apply to the fjords.

Occasionally there are stretches of water, half fjord,

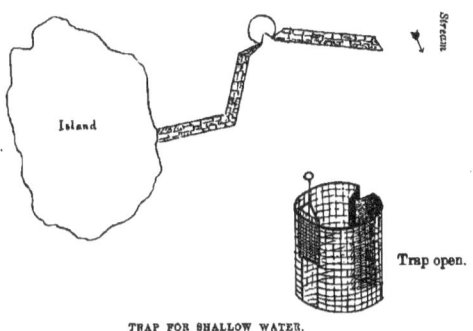

TRAP FOR SHALLOW WATER.

half river, which, however, come under the river regulations, and as these are of no use for angling, the enterprising Norsk uses them as fields for the exercise of his ingenuity in the setting of salmon-traps, and in this pursuit he is no fool.

The trapper selects for his engine a situation where the passage of the fish is narrowly defined, and then extends a projecting arm of timber or masonry to make the

Nets and Traps in the Fjords and Rivers. 37

passage easiest of ascent at one particular point, and at this point he establishes his infernal machine.

Many of these trappers conform to the requirements of the weekly close-time by opening a door at the *upper* end of the trap, thus affording a clear passage for fish through the instrument; but I would oblige them to close the *entrance* to the trap, as I take it that, during close-time, it

A RIVER SALMON-TRAP.

should work neither directly nor indirectly towards the capture of fish.

It stands to reason that fish having passed through the traps during close-time with convenience to themselves, will gain confidence in the structures, and be inclined to continue in their use until they are brought to by the closed door, and meet their fate. Thus the trap, when not fishing, instils a confidence for the benefit of similar other engines, which I maintain should not be, and I am glad to say that river-keepers to whom I have explained my views have fully concurred in them. I would have fixed engines entirely removed during close-time, or, at all events, have the entrances closed, and when convictions are obtained for the illegal use of traps or nets, the engines· should be confiscated in addition to the imposition of the fine.

CHAPTER VII.

THE LAKES OF NORWAY.

THE lakes of Norway are of all sorts and sizes, varying from the little basin at the base of small undulations in the fjelds to large expanses of water several miles in length, fed by rivers or streams supplied by snow or glacier-clad mountains.

In many parts of the country there are chains of lakes connected by links of river which would require years to thoroughly explore. As a rule, they teem with many varieties of Salmonidæ, including salmon, sea-trout, bull-trout, brown and yellow trout, char, and hybrids of these species; and when to this list are added land-locked specimens of the migratory Salmonidæ, it is apparent that an extensive and interesting field is open to the angler and ichthyologist.

Many lakes are let in conjunction with adjacent rivers, while the majority are open to anglers, and, whether open or not, leave to fish them can mostly be obtained by the asking, for the salmon-fisher, except for an odd day or so, has little time or inclination to leave his river in quest of smaller game; thus the lakes are seldom fished by others than those who go out for that especial purpose. The borders of these lakes, and the islands they contain, are favourite resorts of wild-fowl during the breeding season, and it is more than probable that a systematic exploration of these little-frequented inland waters would lead to valuable ornithological discoveries.

An ornithological expedition with the object of discovery of the breeding haunts of wild-fowl could scarcely be combined with an angling tour, for at the nesting-time the fjelds are rotten with half-melted snow, and the scaly inhabitants of the lakes are yet in such poor condition that they offer no attraction to the angler.

The fjeld-lakes are scarcely free from ice until the end of May, and except in a few forward districts, are not worth the angler's attention until well into July; indeed, speaking generally, August is the best month.

Some lakes are simply land-locked basins, others of larger dimensions are fed and relieved by rivers draining considerable tracts of country, and a third description has centuries ago been formed by some huge landslip which has fallen down, and, by blocking up the passage of a river, has created a semi-artificial lake. In the latter description of lake, the overflow may be precipitated over heights not

The Lakes of Norway. 41

negotiable by fish ; whereas, before the date of the landslip, a passage was open to Salmonidæ *viâ* the fjord, the large river and the rivulet, and these accidents of Nature are the key to the solution of many ichthyological puzzles.

Landslips and volcanic disturbances have barred the ascent of fish in many a Norwegian river, but it does not necessarily follow that descent is affected in the same degree, and it is not uncommon to occasionally find a variety of fish in a river which is not general.

Thus the construction and characteristics of the lakes of Norway are of peculiar interest, telling tales of the past, and providing solutions of problems respecting the species of fish they contain at the present day.

It should be noted that the fjeld-lakes have not the same facility to free themselves from winter ice as have the rivers ; and, in consequence, they and their inhabitants require more time to attain condition.

Lakes which communicate with the sea by river and fjord are generally the resort of salmon, sea-trout, and bull-trout for breeding purposes, and it is remarkable that many rivers would be void of spawning redds if it were not for the existence of lakes or lake-like expanses of water at their heads, to which I shall have occasion to refer later on.

Many of the lakes are situated among the fjelds or higher lands of the country ; but it does not necessarily follow that the lakes themselves are at a great altitude above sea-level; they often lie several hundred feet below the ridges which must be crossed to reach them.

In secluded nooks upon the fjelds, and in the sheltered hollows which form the watersheds of the lakes, good pasturage is often found.

These grazing lands are the properties of the hamlets in the valley below; each farmer owns a log house upon his portion of land, called in Norwegian a *sæter*, to which some of his people repair with the cattle so soon as the harvest is garnered in the valley, and will remain there until September or October. These *sæters* may be many miles from the valleys, but the milk is usually sent down to the farm every evening in cask upon horseback, or by bearer.

Many lakes are bordered by trees, and are deep at the sides; but upon those worth fishing a boat is usually to be found.

CHAPTER VIII.

THE COUNTRY-FOLK.

IN previous chapters I have endeavoured to give the reader some idea of the fjelds, rivers, and lakes which combine to constitute the country districts of Norway from the angler's point of view.

This is an easy task as compared with a description of the manners and disposition of her country-folk.

I have been the recipient of much kindness and hospitality at the hands of Norwegian citizens; in fact, so obliging are they to a foreigner that they can scarcely do too much for him.

In some senses, it seems scarcely correct to make use of the word "foreigner," as between Norwegian and British subjects, for their languages, religions, customs, and manners bear such similarity that the inhabitant of Great Britain scarcely feels as if abroad when upon Norwegian soil.

The dwellers upon fjord, fjeld, and riverside have been my partners in sport throughout many a long

A NORWEGIAN FAMILY PARTY.

day and expedition, and I sincerely trust that they have as little fault to find with me as I have with them.

Living as they do from year end to year end in the

The Country-folk.

midst of fish, flesh, and fowl, it would be indeed strange were they not imbued with the love of sport and natural history.

Many of them are true sportsmen in that they possess knowledge of the habits and haunts of beasts, birds, and fish; they know not fatigue, and their patience and perseverance are well-nigh inexhaustible.

I have found the inhabitants of the valleys along the lengthy coast of Norway to differ considerably in disposition and courtesy towards visitors. In some districts they will do all in their power to oblige, and are fair in their dealings, while in others they will not put themselves out of their way to assist, and are somewhat extortionate in their demands.

In the tourist districts, and in the valleys where rivers have been fished for many years, house-rent, wages, and the prices of supplies are fixed; indeed, this is generally the case, but in more remote quarters the country-folk are not above asking for a great deal more than they are prepared to accept.

One cannot expect country-folk to take a great amount of interest in strangers whom, after a few weeks' sojourn, they may never see again; consequently, the casual angler may not be as well treated as one who annually fishes the same river; but the natives of some districts do not appear to grasp the idea that fair dealing and moderate attention may prompt a return visit, or the introduction of others.

To my mind, one of the most pleasing characteristics of the Norwegian peasant is his independence. He is courteous to his neighbours, attends to his own affairs, but gives no homage, and expects none, for all are equal.

During the angling season, the farmers are busy with their crops, and have no inclination to waste their time or yours; they are unaccustomed to attention from one another, and attempts towards affability upon the part of visitors are not understood. They do not bother about one another, and do not expect visitors to bother about them, and I know parts of England where the same feeling exists.

In Norway, the fishing rights of rivers, lakes, and fjords belong to the riparian proprietors, and these cannot be sold apart from the property, but they can be let on lease.

Of late a law has been passed that land cannot be sold to foreigners, the object being to prevent traffic in property which might in the future be required for railway or other purposes, but at present the law applies generally.

The riparian proprietors who own fisheries of small value in somewhat remote districts hear that large rents are obtained for fishing elsewhere. They seldom

The Country-folk.

travel, they know nothing of the sport of angling, and are often ignorant of the comparative value of their own small streams and the better rivers; but, with the arrival of a British visitor, a vision of gold appears before their eyes, and they seldom ask less than their river's worth.

The value of the harvest reaped from sportsmen and tourists is fully appreciated by the Norwegians, and it is to their advantage to know that fair dealing is likely to increase the number of visitors.

The solitary, uneventful life of the valley and the cold and darkness of the protracted winter of their country perhaps incline them to be a trifle phlegmatic, and the disappointments which the vagaries of the short Norwegian summer inflict upon a population chiefly engaged in agriculture, have accustomed them to accept calamity without murmur.

Yet when occasions arise which call for quick resource and prompt action, it is seldom that they are found unequal to the occasion; their remarks and replies are generally to the point, and their wit is distinctly of the dry order. An occasional incident may somewhat excite them, but I am inclined to attribute this to the desire to render the utmost assistance to their companion in sport. Many a time I have been excessively annoyed with myself at the escape of a fish from my hook, but nothing more than a smile flits across my boatman's countenance, and he continues rowing as if nothing had occurred.

When, however, a fish is being played I cannot say he is so steady, and in gaffing a fish he is about the worst hand I have ever met.

It seems quite impossible for him to wait until the gaff can be nicely placed over the shoulder of the fish, he prefers to make wild dashes with the instrument, and frequently succeeds in frightening the fish away, or in gaffing your line.

The rents they make with the gaff deprive me of half the pleasure of the capture, and although I have shown them the correct method times without number, they will be just as clumsy upon the next opportunity, so now I strand my fish whenever possible, and use a net in place of the gaff.

This, however, some do not appreciate, as they think they are deprived of having a hand in the sport. The Norwegian is of kindly disposition, and his care of animals is extreme; in fact, he makes pets of his servants. His knowledge he willingly places at the disposal of his companion in sport, and he will work away with a dogged determination which leaves nothing to be desired. This is the kind of man with whom to go a-fishing. The Norwegian is an adept at all kinds of wood-work, from the building of his house to the manufacture of ropes from twisted twigs, and his knife serves in his deft hands the purposes of half a dozen tools.

THREE LITTLE MAIDS FROM SCHOOL.

CHAPTER IX.

BOATS.

HE Norwegian excels in the craft of wood-working; it is an art peculiarly his own, and in the branch of boat-building he is in the first rank.

It might be expected that a people living upon a sea-board, with water the principal means of transit, should possess boats of superior make and shape, but it is not every nation which in its craft combines the ornamental with the practical.

For use upon the sea, the fjord, and the river, several patterns of boat are in use. There is the boat somewhat of the cutter build, whose prow is but slightly elevated above the height of the gunwale amidships; this is chiefly used for fjord work in proximity to the towns.

The peculiarity of the pattern lies in its gradually decreasing beam from a point rather forward of amidships to the stern; its bottom and sides have considerable flare, and the boat can be whipped from side to side with great facility. The typical boat of the country is built somewhat upon similar lines to the above, but the design is different. From rather forward of amidships she tapers away aft to the bare width of her stern-post, the prow is raised to a considerable height, while the stern is also elevated. Her sides have considerable flare, carried as far forward as possible; thus she sits like a duck upon the water, is of little draught, behaves well in waves or surf, and drags not at all from the stern.

At the present time, oak is employed but to a small extent for boat-building, the pine of the country is in general use. The strakes are about a foot in width, often much more, and these are fastened together by bolts and rivets of galvanized iron, which have superseded the system of pegging with wood.

The boat is either oiled, or painted with Stockholm tar, and with ordinary care will last for years.

The oars and sculls are also made of pine, and are innocent of buttons.

The fulcrum is a single rowlock of pine, and a loop of cord or twisted birch-twig running through a hole in the gunwale is passed over the handle of the oar, serving to keep it more or less in position when out of hand, and providing a fulcrum when it is desired to backwater.

The rudder is hung upon iron pins, and is controlled by a tiller usually formed of two rods jointing at right angles; but for inland and angling purposes no rudder is used.

As already stated, the native boat is of very light draught, and can easily be hauled or "tracked" up-stream, no matter how shallow may be the water, and likewise can with safety be run upon shallows or the bank when a fish has to be landed. It is an excellent boat for angling.

The largest rivers of Norway are fishable only by boat; the lower and middle waters of the medium-size rivers, in some of their pools, are certain to require a boat, and even the small rivers require this accessory more frequently than the angler might wish.

Somehow or another, unless the catch can be commanded from the bank of big waters, a boat is mostly necessary, as there is generally such an expanse of deepish water between the bank and the catch as places wading out of the question, and, in many cases, the rough bottom and powerful stream prohibit the practice.

In the uppermost pools of the larger rivers, and throughout the small rivers, the waders can be used with advantage; but under a broiling hot sun I personally prefer to wade without them.

The boats, when not in use, are moored to the bank upon the easy side of the stream, or up some convenient backwater, but when it is desired to leave the boat upon some strand, the native system is to pull the boat up, fasten the painter to the largest adjacent stone, and pile upon and around the latter sufficient other stones as will securely anchor the boat should a rise of water take place, occasioned either by rainfall or melted snow—this precaution should never be omitted, especially in situations where a rise of a foot or so is sufficient to flood a considerable area. Acquaintance with the methods of the Norwegian brings the conviction that he is hard to beat at his own game.

An excellent boat for angling purposes costs but the equivalent to from 28*s.* to 35*s.*, and in some places even less, and such, with ordinary attention, will last for ten years or more. These boats are in every respect superior to those built in Great Britain for angling work, and can be held with ease in rapid water. I use them at home in preference to our boats.

For fishing lakes a sea-anchor will be found of great service, especially when the angler has no attendant. By its aid the boat is kept head to wind as she drifts at a suitable pace for casting. To hold a fishing-boat a sea-anchor of sail area 18 ins. square is quite sufficient.

CHAPTER X.

SALMONIDÆ OF NORWAY.

THE list of Salmonidæ found in Norway includes the following distinct species, viz. the salmon, sea-trout, bull-trout, yellow trout, brown trout, grayling, and char, which, when existing under normal conditions, differ little in characteristics from the various species common to the British Isles.

The inhabitants of the various rivers and lakes possess slight peculiarities in shape, colouring, and marking, as is also the case in rivers of other countries; but these should rarely give the ichthyologist serious trouble in identification.

It will have been gathered from a perusal of the previous chapters that from mountain summit to river bed, the *country* of Norway is far *bigger* than that of the British Isles, and, in consequence of the climate, the chapter of accidents which affects fish-rearing and fish-life is proportionately longer and more varied.

Acquaintance with this less conventional land reveals the purport and value of many provisions of Nature, which may scarcely seem necessary for the protection and perpetuation of animal life in Great Britain, and reminds the observer how circumscribed is his own little sphere. In rivers and lakes, which at certain portions of their courses have at one time or another been pretty well turned upside down, it is not very remarkable that curiosities of fish-life should abound, yet in the large majority of cases a careful examination of the subject will lead to certain identification with a distinct species at some stage of the latter's existence, although the size of the curiosity may be abnormal.

In a country where the ordinary journeys of migratory Salmonidæ are possibly held in suspense for months or years, by effects of climate or convulsions of Nature, it may be not unwise, in the first stages of examination, to dismiss the size of the subject from calculation, and to commence with the application of the tests for species; then, should this result in a solution of the problem, the causes of individual peculiarity are ripe for speculation or further investigation.

It is not probable that every angler will take sufficient interest to study all the details of fish-life, and, as the discovery of an uncommon object appears to possess a fascination, a tendency would unfortunately seem to exist which invests a rather unusual specimen with an interest to which in reality it has no claim.

I have frequently had specimens presented with the query, "What's this?" the exhibitor evidently expecting a reply which would suggest some rare object; but it seldom has been other than one showing a trifling variety in shape or colour from some accepted species.

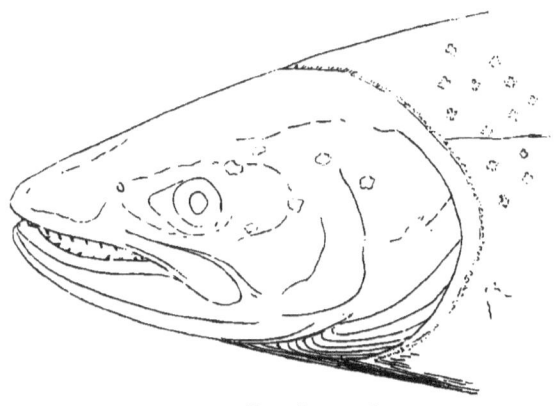

SALMON, 5] LBS. (⅔ LIFE-SIZE).

The inquirer generally seems disappointed, so to dissipate such illusions is no tasteful task; but the ruthless knife of the surgeon must be conscientiously applied in the interests of natural history.

To assist in the identification of salmon (*Salmo salar*), sea-trout (*Salmo trutta*), bull-trout (*Salmo eriox*), and

SOME SALMONIDÆ AND THEIR CHARACTERISTICS.

Species.	Shape and Scales.	Colour.	Marking.	Gill-covers.	Teeth.	Fins.	Tail.
TROUT— (*Salmo fario*) (Norsk—*Ørret*).	Head: rather round and blunt at nose. Body: somewhat lumpy in outline as compared with S. trutta and S. salar. Scales: brilliant when in condition.	Brown on back, shading lighter to medial line, sides yellow, and belly white.	Black and red spots situated without reference to medial line, gradually decreasing in number from a point half-way down the body.	Outline irregular, generally an angle at level of medial line. Freely spotted without reference to medial line. (*See Plates.*)	Upper jaw: two rows. Under jaw: one row. Vomer: one row, alternately setting outwards. Tongue: two rows. (*See Plate.*)	Dorsal: brown, spotted with black. Adipose: brown, the tip spotted with disc of orange to red. Pectoral: orange. Ventral: orange. Anal: orange, *lowest ray white*.	Forked, but less so with age. The outlines are convex.
SEA-TROUT— (*Salmo trutta*) (Norsk—*Sjø-ørret*).	Head: small, clean-shaped. Body: even and elegant in outline. Scales: lustrous and silvery.	Bright and silvery, dark-green on back, shading lighter to silver flanks, and white belly.	Freely marked with black cross-shaped spots from back to medial line, more sparsely so to a short distance below. Some spots are rather square in shape.	Outline regular and oval, sparsely spotted. (*See Plates.*)	Upper jaw: two rows. Under jaw: one row. Vomer: two rows, each setting outwards and disappearing in old age. Tongue: two rows. (*See Plate.*)	Slate colour to white. Dorsal fin: spotted or blotched with black.	Forked, the inside edges being little rounded. (*See Plate.*)
BULL-TROUT— (*Salmo eriox*) (Norsk—*Græs-ørret*).	Head: clumsy. Body: bulky in shape and inelegant. Scales: of the brightness of fresh-cut lead rather than silver. Not lustrous.	Of rather leaden shade. Back: green shading to white flanks and belly.	Freely spotted with black marks, square in shape, without regard to medial line, but some fish have few spots below it. Before first visit to sea, spotted with black and red marks.	Round in outline and irregular, especially in the males. Freely spotted. (*See Plates.*)	Upper jaw: two rows. Under jaw: one row. Vomer: one row. Tongue: one row. (*See Plates.*)	Dorsal: brown-green, blotched black. Adipose: slate, orange at tip. Pectoral: orange. Ventral: fore visit to sea, slate to white; after first visit to sea, slate to white. Anal: slate to white.	When young, roundly forked. When old, square. Very old, convex. (*See Plate.*)
SALMON— (*Salmo salar*) (Norsk—*Lax*).	Body: elegant in outline. Head: small and of thoroughbred shape. Scales: silvery and lustrous.	Back: dark-green, shading to medial line. Steel-blue shade just above medial line. Flanks: silvery white. Belly: lustrous white.	Spotted black, of design from cross to square marks. Very few, if any, spots below medial line, but a few immediately behind gill-cover in some cases.	Regular and round in outline. Those of males are more irregular than in outline. Sparsely spotted. (*See Plate.*)	Upper jaw: two rows. Under jaw: one row, extremities toothless. Vomer: cluster of teeth at point. Tongue: two rows. Thorax: Upper, two rows. Lower, one row. (*See Plates.*)	Dorsal } slate colour. Adipose } Pectoral } Ventral } light slate to Anal } white.	Forked, getting less so with age, and when old quite square.

N.B.—These particulars apply to fish in good condition.

[*To face p.* 57.

Salmonidæ of Norway.

common trout (*Salmo fario*), the annexed table will be found in convenient form for reference, and contains mention of the points by which the different species are distinguishable.

As regards curious specimens, landlocked fish, etc., I will allude to those I have seen in Norway in the following pages.

SALMON (*Salmo salar*; Norsk, *Lax*).

Shape.—Body, elegant in outline; head, small and thoroughbred.

Scales.—Lustrous and silvery.

Colour.—Back, dark green shading lighter, then blueish tinge.

Flanks, silvery white.

Belly, lustrous white.

Marking.—Spotted black, the spots being in shape from cross to square. Few if any spots below medial line, except immediately behind gill-covers.

Gill-covers.—Regular and round in outline. Those of males are more irregular. Sparsely spotted.

Teeth.—Upper jaw, two rows } extremities toothless.
Lower jaw, one row

Vomer, cluster of teeth at point.

Tongue, two rows.

Thorax: upper, two rows; lower, one row.

Angling Travels in Norway.

Fins.—Dorsal, adipose, and pectoral, slate-colour.
Ventral and anal, light slate to white.

Tail.—Forked, less so with age; square when old; colour, slate.

Previous to my acquaintance with the fjords, rivers, and lakes of Norway, I had been given to understand that,

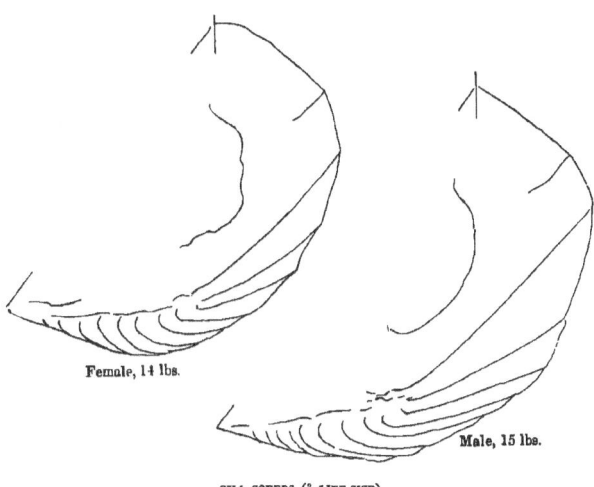

GILL-COVERS (⅔ LIFE-SIZE).

broadly speaking, the salmon of the country was a gamer fish to kill and less tasteful as food than his brethren of the British Isles, but my own experience shows that he is neither better nor worse in either respect; in fact,

Salmonidæ of Norway. 59

he proved to be exactly what I expected to find him.

The salmon affords the most sport and the best food the nearer to the sea he be captured ; and, *vice versâ*, he becomes of less value for both purposes as he wends his way to the spawning-beds.

Some rivers of Norway communicate directly with the sea, others discharge their waters into fjords vary-

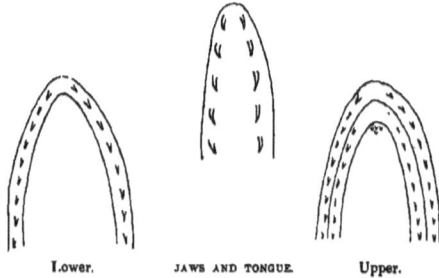

Lower.   JAWS AND TONGUE.   Upper.

ing in length from five to forty or more miles, and in accordance with the distance that the fish have to travel before capture, their value for sport and food should be gauged.

The waters of the fjords are sufficiently brackish to grow seaweed, and mature sea-fish, such as codling, whiting, etc., to within a few yards of their inland extremities, and it is but natural that salmon, while navigating such favourable waters, should lose less in condition than if the journey were performed in fresh water, to all intents and purposes devoid of food.

As salmon commence to lose condition upon their departure from the sea, it is fair to argue that they lose the same in a proportion as the water becomes less saline, and contains less food in the way of small fish.

It is a fact that salmon feed largely upon the herring, and in many districts the reason of the scarcity of fish  in the river is explained by the natives by their loitering in the fjords after food; but when such excuses have been made, the fishing has subsequently been indifferent, and my opinion is that by the time the salmon leaves the sea for the fjord he is in perfect condition, and his business is to seek the spawning-grounds, consequently I pay little heed to the herring-detaining theory.

The salmon is intent upon the business he has immediately in hand, whether it be feeding, running, or breeding. When he is feeding—I mean in the sea—he is rarely seen; when he is running he rarely, if ever, feeds; and when he is on the redds he bestows not a glance or thought upon other matters.

When we have had no fish in the river, I cannot remember that many were being caught in the fjord

Salmonidæ of Norway.

unless perhaps at the very junction with the sea, so I think salmon run through the fjords without loss of time.

Salmon from a distance of many scores of miles become aware that their river is open to them by the same incomprehensible senses which inform wild-fowl of the exact date when their northern resorts, hundreds of miles away, are free from ice and ripe for visitation; and these acute senses—usually described as instinct—remind one of the behaviour of cattle on board ship when approaching land not yet in sight.

I should say that the average weight of the salmon killed in Norway is greater than the same in the British Isles, as in many of the largest and medium-size rivers, fish weighing over 30 lbs. are, comparatively speaking, common, and I do not hesitate to say that in the lowest and middle stretches of rivers they take a suitable bait more freely.

The angler, upon his first visit to Norwegian waters, will be surprised at how seldom fish show themselves in the pools; they, however, frequently jump immediately they have ascended a stream, as is the case in our own rivers.

During the first four weeks or so of an average season in Norway, the rivers are maintained at a height favourable for "running," for reasons before mentioned, and under such circumstances the British angler would expect fish to "take" freely, and from my personal experience

I should not wonder at a scarcity of "jumpers," as I generally find that the jumping fish, by external appearance, have been some time in the river, while the fresh-run ones that I kill frequently have made no display before taking the lure.

I counted the fin rays of two fish killed in the Sürendal river (the Surna) upon the 23rd and 25th July. The fish each weighed 17 lbs., and the rays were as follows:—

Dorsal fin	13 rays
Anal ,,	11 ,,
Pectoral ,,	14 ,,
Ventral ,,	9 ,,
Caudal ,,	19 ,,

In one of the fish the last ray of the dorsal fin was very short, with appearance of having been injured.

I have met with a few fish of the hog-backed type, some fish with rather large, and others with rather small tails; but these peculiarities are not uncommon in British waters, and the skin readily becomes tinted with whatever colouring matter a water may contain.

There are early and late rivers in Norway, and in accordance with the date of the ascent of the fish, the spawning-time may approximately be determined.

In some of the early rivers in the North, the fish become red by the middle of July, and upon the 24th of that month I have killed new fish as full-bellied as are those of the Solway rivers about the end of October, and from my own experience I should say that the average date of spawning in Norwegian rivers is from a month to six weeks earlier than the average of Great Britain.

The angling season closes generally upon September 15, and the spawning operations commence within a few weeks' time, so the fish can reckon upon a full month at least during which the ova and milt can be deposited ere the surface of those rivers which freeze over will become ice-covered.

Some rivers in the south of Norway, and many further north which flow out of lakes, are free of ice throughout winter, but upon others the water running over thin shallows is often frozen in patches right through, and some situations which have been selected as redds may be left high and dry as the river falls in, and the percentage of ova lost from these causes is far greater than in a less rigorous climate, while the voracious bull-trout ever exacts toll. There is also a considerable formation of ground-ice in many rivers which is undesirable in a hatchery, and the open ones run extremely dry.

In consequence of the low temperature of these rivers, the regulation period of ninety days required for hatching the ova is probably often exceeded, except where the rivers are fed by warm springs.

Allowing a liberal period for the deposit of ova, the fish should be hatched out by the end of February, and by the time of the clearance of ice the youngsters should have absorbed the contents of the yolk-bag, and have become perfect fish.

At this time, and throughout the season, the parr may be observed feeding in the backwaters, or stationed in some miniature stream formed by stones at the margin of the river, where for the first few weeks he fattens upon particles scarcely visible to the human eye.

Later on, he devotes his attention to midges, and then to fair-sized flies, until the winter again comes round, and his appetite can only be satisfied by subaquæous food.

The parr differ in size to much the same extent as in British rivers, so it is probable that their transformation into smolts is governed by the same laws as are proved to exist in the British Isles; indeed, the provision of Nature, which ordains that half of each brood should remain as parr for two years, would seem to be of extreme value in this land of accident, in order to preserve a portion of each year's production.

At the commencement of June, I have seen salmon-fry an inch to an inch-and-a-half long, and on the first of July I have seen them two-and-a-half inches in length disporting themselves in the rivers and fresh-water portions of the fjords.

Salmonidæ of Norway.

In the first instance, I was considerably perplexed to account for the absence of smolts in Norwegian rivers, and in order to ascertain if they were taking shelter up the backwaters and small streams, I for many days took a trout rod with me, and for an hour or so whipped all likely places, but only succeeded in hooking trout and parr.

I have seen large numbers of smolts just below the entrance of rivers into the fjords, but in the rivers themselves I have not seen a single specimen.

I have been shown as smolts fish which really were parr or trout, and I have been informed that smolts were in abundance upon the higher reaches of the river. I have been fishing at the time, and throughout a period of two months they have not passed down, and I have arrived at the conclusion that the smolts descend the river before the commencement of the salmon-angling season, probably at, or very soon after, the break-up of winter, and when the early date at which the ova is shed and the late opening of the angling season are taken into consideration, it is not surprising that the smolts should have departed seawards by the first week in June.

In the small rivers grilse will run up early; but in the large rivers, and even in many small ones, the arrival of the grilse heralds the close of salmon angling.

By about the middle of July the rivers become small (unless there should be rain), and the grilse take to the river, appropriating for resting-places the very rocks and stones which, in bigger waters, were shelters for salmon; they freely take the fly or minnow, and fight well.

For the first month or so of the angling season, when the melting snow and ice throughout the highlands of the watershed maintain the rivers in good ply, salmon keep running up with every tide, naturally gaining the rivers in greater numbers during the weekly close-time for netting; but when the snow is exhausted, a few will run up only during the close-time, or if there be rain.

From the commencement of the angling season the rivers are remarkably free of kelts; indeed, these are as scarce as smolts, and, in my opinion, for one and the same reason.

I calculate that the smolt is prepared to descend the rivers early in May, while the kelt certainly is so, and both desire a flood to permit of their departure; thus, as water sufficient for the purpose is certain to occur at latest soon after the end of April, both smolt and kelt take advantage of the first opportunity.

I am certain that in some waters of the British Isles the existence of smolts causes delay in the return of kelts to the sea, and by the early removal of smolts the inducement does not exist.

The pylorics of the salmon fresh from the sea, via fjord and river, are extended with fat, or perhaps I should say with essence of food, the individual strings of these organs having the appearance of being merged into one mass; a layer of this nutritious extract underlies the skin, and intervenes between the flakes of solid flesh, the secretion being more abundant in the neighbourhood of the abdomen.

The consumer appreciates the difference between the rich and lean portions of the salmon, and, if he be wise, would select the "thick" or the "thin" in accordance with his powers of digestion.

In this manner the salmon carries sufficient supplies to sustain him during an existence of comparative inactivity, and adequate to meet the demands of ova or milt.

The supply of food in a salmon river is so limited that it would not pay for the working; and I think that, to all intents and purposes, salmon do not feed in the river; I have most carefully examined the internal economy of scores of fish, and have found nothing in the stomach beyond a greenish liquid and a few reddish, shelly fragments, which I have recognized as the cases of the freshwater shrimp.

I will not go so far as to say that the unspawned salmon will not feed in fresh water of a river; very likely he would, if there were sufficient food to pay for the hunting, but in that case there would be no necessity for the secretive organs and tissues which he possesses.

If a salmon were to attempt to gain subsistence solely from the food which exists in a river he would wear himself to skin and bone in the process; but the same exertion is not required in picking up fragments which pass under his very nose as he rests upon the river-bed.

The stomach of the salmon, with its ducts and exit, becomes contracted by disuse when in the river, and the small particles of food which he obtains merely perform the office of keeping the machinery from absolute inaction.

I have opened fish whose stomachs contained small white worms, and in many others I have found the tapeworm. From the proportions of a certain cock fish, I put him down as a forty-pounder, but upon weighing him I was astonished to find that he drew the scale at but thirty pounds. I tried another steel-yard with the same reading. His frame was certainly that of a fish nigh upon forty pounds, but a further inspection showed him to be narrow.

Upon opening him we discovered a large tape-worm, and thus the mystery was revealed, for he had been supporting a lodger. The existence of tape-worm in salmon is far from uncommon in Norway.

I have frequently found sea-lice upon fish which have negotiated from thirty to forty miles of fjord, and beyond that fifteen miles of river, but when captured at the mouth of a river such a distance from the sea the parasites are not very numerous, nor are they very firmly

Salmonidæ of Norway.

attached to the fish, and by the time that ten to fifteen miles of river have been travelled but few lice will remain; in fact the brackish and fresh water seem to affect salmon and sea-lice alike.

In a big water, both in British and Norwegian rivers, the salmon will run up during the daytime, for they may frequently be seen jumping at the stream-tops after having negotiated the rapid water below; but, in lower states of the water, I think this practice is more general with the Norwegian salmon, and I have frequently observed three or four ascending together through water scarcely three feet in depth, illuminated by a midday sun.

The long Norwegian twilight will allow the angler to continue operations until eleven or twelve o'clock throughout the month of June, and as far north as Bergen there is sufficient light to fish comfortably until 9 p.m. up to about August 10. The habits of the fish doubtless are affected by the light as regards "taking," especially in low waters, but, by common consent, they appear to desist from "taking" at some variable hour which, in my opinion, is determined by the daily or nightly temperature and light.

If the evening be warm and balmy, salmon will often take up to midnight; but, on the other hand, should cold atmosphere or wind set in, it is of little good to continue fishing after 7 or 8 p.m.; in fact, in cold weather, I much prefer the daytime.

Many British and Norwegian anglers decry fishing under a hot sun, but in heavy waters I think it makes not much difference, and even in small waters I have done very well if the sun does not shine down-stream.

I have been frequently warned, when starting out under a sun beating straight down upon the river, that I was not very likely to raise a fish, and my boatman, or gaffer, has implored me to wait until five o'clock in the evening, but with plenty of water I generally pay little attention to sun in Norway, and have nothing to regret for my waywardness, principally thanking the free-taking habits of the Norwegian salmon.

There is only one direction of the sun upon the river during which I decline to fish, and that is when it strikes down a pool, and, consequently, straight into the eyes of fish, thus the general direction of a river's course is of much importance in day-angling.

In various parts of Norway a fairly extensive system of marking fish and returning them to the water has been practised, with the object of advancement of our knowledge of the natural history of the salmon, with the result that fish have very seldom been recaptured south of the river in which they were originally taken, while, upon the other hand, they have frequently been caught north of it, which suggests the inference that kelts, upon regaining salt water, are in the habit of travelling in a northern direction. The

Salmonidæ of Norway.

details have been published by the Norwegian Inspector of Fisheries, and are invested with no mean value.

There is a theory—or, perhaps, I may say a belief—among the sea-fishermen that the salmon feed upon the herrings, and follow them into the fjords; and several have told me that they have frequently seen salmon disgorging herrings when confined in the nets. These statements, which I believe to be reliable, combined with authenticated instances of herrings having been actually found in the stomachs of salmon in our own country, would seem to leave little room for doubt, at all events, as to one article of their diet.

There are many rivers in Norway which are headed by a single lake, others which spring from a chain of lakes with insufficient facilities between them for the passage of salmon; and, again, there are rivers intersected by lakes through which the fish freely run.

It is frequently the case that the communications between lakes of which the salmon makes use become, for all practical purposes, cut off, as the season wanes, and it follows that the fish who occupy the uppermost lakes are the first to ascend the river. Later on, the lower lakes, should there be any, become stocked with fish, and so the available space becomes occupied.

The Norwegian lakes are mostly very deep in the middle portions (I have let out 150 yards of loaded line without reaching the bottom), and the fish frequent the shallower water near the sides, usually selecting a site near a promontory, to obtain whatever stream the lake may afford.

To satisfy my curiosity, I have netted such portions, and have ascertained that fish which have run up at the beginning of June have by July 15 become very discoloured, and the milt or ova so far advanced in condition that spawning should commence within about six weeks' time. At the commencement of spawning operations, the fish draw up the rivers and tributaries or towards the edges of the lakes, and dig troughs out of stones and rubble within sight of an observer upon the bank, selecting a locality which possesses some little stream or current.

Salmon seem to become lethargic upon entering the lakes, and I have rarely seen them jump except soon after their entrance at the outlet, and it is difficult to tempt them with fly or bait.

Herr Landmark, the Government Inspector of Fisheries in Norway, publishes periodically his reports, which, in addition to providing us with much information of great value as regards statistics, supply us with the results of an extended system of experiment conducted by himself and others, notably by Mr. Walter E. Archer, the present Inspector of Salmon Fisheries of Scotland.

As a practical ichthyologist, he warns us that his

Salmonidæ of Norway.

experiments and systems have not yet been conducted upon so large a scale as to render it absolutely safe to accept the results of his labours as facts in the general natural history of the Salmo salar of Norway.

As an individual, I am prepared to accept the result of their experiments as conclusive evidence upon many points; and persons more difficult to convince must admit that the many straws they have tracked at least tend to show the direction in which the wind blows. Herr Landmark's experiments in marking salmon have proved that, as a general rule, fish return to spawn in the river of their birth. Of 56 fish marked in a certain river, 34 were recaught in it, 1 in a different river, and 22 by nets at distances varying from half a mile to 200 miles from where marked.*

Herr Landmark points out that Salmo salar while at sea travels with the current, and as this sets northwards during summer along the western coast of Norway, it follows that the more northern rivers benefit by those southern-bred fish which get somewhat beyond their reckoning in search of food, and of others which prefer to strike another river rather than await with great inconvenience to themselves a rise in the temperature of their native stream.

* *Vide* Annual Report of the Fishery Board for Scotland for 1892, Part II., note 11.

Herr Landmark says that the river Aaensira furnishes somewhat of an exception to the rule that fish in a large majority of instances return to their native rivers, and he explains that the temperature of this river in spring and early summer is exceptionally low; but this river affords no *great* exception to the rule, for of fifteen fish marked and subsequently recovered, twelve were recaptured in or close to the river itself, and of the other three, one was recaptured 200 miles, another 230 miles, and the third 500 miles, all north of the Aaensira.

There would appear to be no particular reason why a fish should seek "fresh fields and pastures new," if he can satisfy his requirements close at hand under conditions favourable to his existence and to his advance towards maturity. Herr Landmark says that of the fish marked, 36 per cent. were males, whereas of those recaptured the males represented the proportion of 11 per cent., and he suggests that this decrease in the percentage of males may be accounted for by the great mortality which occurs among cock fish after spawning. Perhaps the more wary and cunning nature of the male fish renders him less liable to be captured a second time either by rod or net, and any one who knows much about nets and the netting of fish can testify that fish recognize them at a glance, and take advantage of the slightest loophole to effect their escape.

Salmonidæ of Norway.

The result of the marking of fish in Norway shows that no hard-and-fast rule can be made as regards the increase in weight of fish from one year to another; in fact, as in most points concerning the natural history of the salmon, we must not pay too much attention to exceptions, but rather base our calculations upon the general average.

Herr Landmark says that fish weighing from 1½ to 3 kgs. in one year increase on an average 100 per cent.; fish of from 3 to 5 kgs. increase 50 per cent.; fish of from 5 to 7 kgs. increase 40 per cent.; fish from 7 to 9 kgs. increase 25 per cent.; and, lastly, fish of from 9 to 12 kgs. increase 20 per cent., which means that a fish of 27 lbs. would increase in weight about 5½ lbs. in a single year, which, more or less, agrees with the calculations of experts in this country as regards British salmon.

It must be remembered that a 27 lb. fish will lose from 4 to 5 lbs. in weight during spawning, and in the course of a year he regains this loss of 4 to 5 lbs., and increases in weight to another 5 lbs. or so, making a total increase of about 10 lbs. between the kelt stage and the date when he next ascends the river as a fresh fish.

The last question I shall attempt to deal with in regard to the salmon is, how often does he spawn?

I must again revert to Herr Landmark's investigations,

which prove that thirteen salmon which were marked in one year, either when in condition just ready for spawning, or immediately after they had spawned, were retaken the following year in similar condition.

It is pretty generally admitted in Norway that a large number of fish which spawn in the lower reaches of a river will fall back to the sea before winter, and as the spawning takes place fairly early, such fish would have ample time to regain condition, and again ascend the river in the following June or July, so there would appear to be no reason why such fish should not spawn annually.

On the other hand, it is well known that large numbers of salmon remain in the rivers until spring, and these are named "winter fish," and I cannot believe that such fish, descending in spring, with a long journey before them, can have sufficient time to regain condition and increase in weight so that they can reascend the rivers before autumn or late in summer.

It may be argued that the "winter fish," which we will say descend in April and May, would have sufficient time to reattain condition and occupy the lower redds of the river in September; then, having spawned, may drop down to the sea before winter, and come up again as spring fish in June. By such a system, fish would spawn high up and low down the river in alternate years; but this cannot be the case as far as concerns the rivers I have fished, for

Salmonidæ of Norway.

in these the big fish invariably run up very early when there is plenty of water, and as the volume of water decreases so does the size of the fish running up.

In Great Britain, the rivers are such that, with favourable waters, fish can run throughout the twelve months; but it by no means follows that a fish ascends to breed every year; it is common for spring fish to ascend the river in the winter and spring months, and those that avoid an untimely end spawn, say, in December, and descend the river in March, April, and May of the following spring, about a year after they came up.

In rivers which have both autumn and spring "runs," it is possible that fish descending in spring may re-ascend in autumn, then they would be spring and autumn fish in alternate years; but I fail to see how fish can breed annually in British or any other rivers which only have a spring run, *i.e.* so long as they pass the winter in the river.

To revert to Norwegian fisheries—as an instance, I will take the Salten river. The run of fish has practically ended early in August, at which date I have observed many fish far advanced towards spawning condition in the topmost cascade-like pools of the Junkerdal river, which, at its junction with the Lons river at Storjord, is named the Salten river. These fish are breeding at a distance of about a hundred miles from the sea proper, and I am of opinion that it is impossible for them to shed their ova, or milt, in late autumn, then to visit the sea in early spring, and return to the river in June or July, having in the interim traversed two hundred miles, regained about 5 lbs. lost in the kelt stage, and have accumulated an additional increase in weight of 5 lbs. at the least.

If Salmo salar can spawn annually under such conditions as these, he must pass the majority of his days in racing up and down the river and fjord.

Some instances have been recorded of fish marked as kelts in spring having been recaptured as fresh-run fish in autumn, but this would be impossible in rivers which afford insufficient water for an autumn "run."

The conclusions I arrive at are—

(1) That salmon which have spawned in pools which in the autumn have open communication with the fjord or sea, may, and frequently do, return to the sea after spawning and before winter, and under such conditions may very well spawn each year.

(2) That salmon which have spawned in situations from which no departure is possible until the following spring, may spawn each year, provided that their river admits of an autumn "run."

Salmonidæ of Norway.

(3) That salmon which have spawned in situations from which departure is impossible until the following spring, in a river which has no autumn run, spawn but once in two years.

(4) That fish which ascend the rivers each autumn can well spawn each year.

(5) That fish can spawn each year in rivers which admit of both spring and autumn "runs," provided that the fish do not confine themselves to either spring or autumn "running."

(6) That fish which descend the rivers as kelts in winter (December and January) can reascend as fresh fish in the following summer (July and later).

I call attention to these points, as, if I am correct, they bear somewhat strongly upon the system of breeding from "spring" or "autumn" fish, and upon the *annual* growth of the salmon.

The results derived from the marking of fish by Mr. Walter E. Archer, than whom there exists no greater authority upon the natural history of Norwegian salmon, are most instructive, both as regards the facts they prove and the inferences to be drawn from them.

In the Suldal (or Sand's river), the Aaensira, the Figgen, and the Topdals rivers, of some thousands of fish marked, 56 were recaptured.

Of these 56 fish—

> Four may be dismissed on account of accident or uncertainty.
>
> One was marked on December 18, 1886, as fresh-run, and was recaptured in August, 1887, as "apparently" a kelt, 18 lbs. and 16 lbs. being the respective weights.
>
> One was marked in December as a kelt of $9\frac{1}{4}$ lbs., and was recaught in the following April, still a kelt weighing 9 lbs.
>
> One was marked in December "about to spawn," weight 15 lbs., and was recaught in the following April, weight $10\frac{1}{2}$ lbs. a kelt.
>
> One was marked in December as "about to spawn," weight 19 lbs., and was recaught as a kelt in the following April, weight 13 lbs.
>
> Eighteen were marked either as kelts or fish about to spawn (13 being kelts and 5 being fish about to spawn), and all of these were recaught either as kelts or fish about to spawn in the breeding season immediately following that in which they were first marked.
>
> Thirty were marked either as kelts or as fish ascending the river to spawn, and were not recaught until the *second* season after they had been marked.

Nothing was recorded of their proceedings for an entire season.

Thus of 48 fish marked and recaptured, it is proved that 18 spawned twice in consecutive breeding seasons, and that 30 fish spawned one season, that nothing was seen of them during the next season, but that during the second season after marking they were recaptured as kelts or fish about to spawn.

These 30 fish may have spawned or may not have spawned in the season during which nothing is recorded of them; but, as Mr. Walter E. Archer points out, there is negative evidence in favour of their having missed a season.

Fish remaining in the sea from twelve to eighteen months at a time would be expected to gain more in weight per annum than those which spawn annually, and we have here the fact that these 30 fish which, so to say, were lost sight of for an entire season, gained half as much again in weight per annum as compared with the 18 fish which spawned annually for two years.

Again, of the marked fish, on account of the risks run by fish and labels, it would have appeared probable that more would have been recovered during the first season after marking than in later years, but the opposite has been the case—18 fish having been recaught during the first season after marking, whereas 30 fish were recaptured during the second year after marking.

I may also draw attention to the fact that of the 18 fish which spawned in two successive years, about one-half reascended the river during the second year in the month of July, and the other half in the late autumn, whereas of the 30 fish which did or did not miss a season, 22 reascended the river in May, June, and July, and 8 in October and November.

I fully expect that experiments in the future will prove that many fish breed but once in two years, much in accordance with the laws of nature, which rule that of a brood of parr, one-half becomes smolts at one year of age, and the other half at two years.

The annexed sketches were taken from Norwegian fish.

SEA-TROUT (*Salmo trutta*; Norsk, *Søørret*).

Shape.—Head, small and refined; body, even and elegant in outline.

Scales.—Silvery and lustrous.

Colour.—Bright and silvery; back, dark green, shading lighter to silver flanks and lustrous white belly.

Marking.—Freely marked with black, cross-shaped spots from back to medial line; more sparsely spotted from medial line to short distance below. Some spots are rather square in shape.

Gill-covers.—Oval and regular in outline. Sparsely spotted.

Salmonidæ of Norway. 83

Teeth.—Upper jaw, two rows.

    Under jaw, one row.

    Vomer, two rows, setting outwards (these disappear with age, and only a few remain at point of jaw).

    Tongue, two rows.

Fins.—Slate-colour to white.

    Dorsal, spotted or blotched with black.

Tail.—Forked, the inside edges being little rounded; colour, slate.

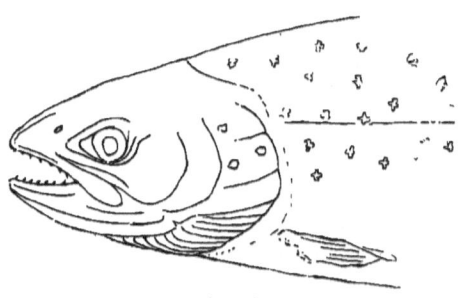

SEA-TROUT, 2 LBS. (⅜ LIFE-SIZE).

The sea-trout is common throughout the greater part of Norway, and shares the large and smaller rivers with his relation the salmon, while in the smallest rivers he only meets with the trout.

The date of his entry of a river, in the same manner as that of the salmon, is governed by the temperature of the water; consequently, his ascent commences at times varying with the nature of the watersheds of various rivers; but, as I have observed that in the larger rivers the advent of the sea-trout is from two to three weeks later than that of the salmon, I believe he requires a higher temperature of water.

In the small rivers, which are soon clear of snow-water,

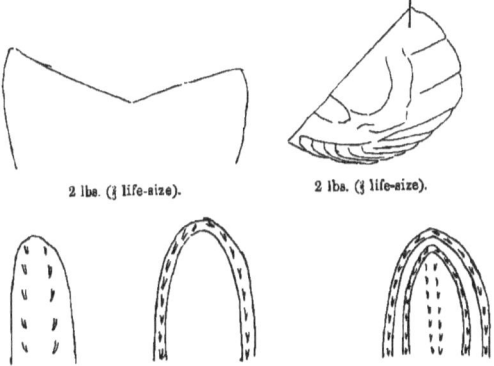

2 lbs. (⅓ life-size).   2 lbs. (⅓ life-size).

TAIL, GILL-COVER, TONGUE, AND JAWS.

and are early in the season warmed by the sun's rays, the sea-trout will run during the first week in June; but in some of the smaller glacier-fed rivers their ascent takes place at a later date.

The size of the sea-trout has great variety upon different Norwegian rivers; the ordinary weight will be

Salmonidæ of Norway.

from about 2 to 6 lbs. ; but upon many rivers, especially those running into the Nord fjord, they grow to an immense size ; 10 lbs. is no uncommon weight, and each season will reveal fish of this size up to 16 lbs., or even more.

The size and character of various rivers in Norway combine to make them suitable for the requirements of sea-trout or salmon, and frequently both species are found in one river, yet it does not follow that they will thrive equally well in a single water ; indeed, facts seem to suggest the contrary.

Rivers prolific in salmon of great weight are not always remarkable for the size of the sea-trout, and those which produce the largest sea-trout are not the most celebrated for salmon of vast proportions ; hence it would appear that although sea-trout can thrive fairly well in large salmon rivers, the smaller ones would seem more favourable to their existence and spawning operations.

I have found sea-trout in the smaller rivers at the commencement of June, but in the larger rivers I have not noted their arrival until about three weeks later than that of the salmon.

The sea-trout appear to run up the rivers in schools for a certain distance from the mouth, and then they gradually separate and seek the tributaries, which they will penetrate so far as the water will allow.

I have frequently met the first run of these fish when casting down to the tail of a salmon-pool subsiding into thin water running over a gravelly bottom. There is no mistaking the sea-trout's style of play, and the fun is fast and furious as one after another attacks the angler's fly; nevertheless, should this sport

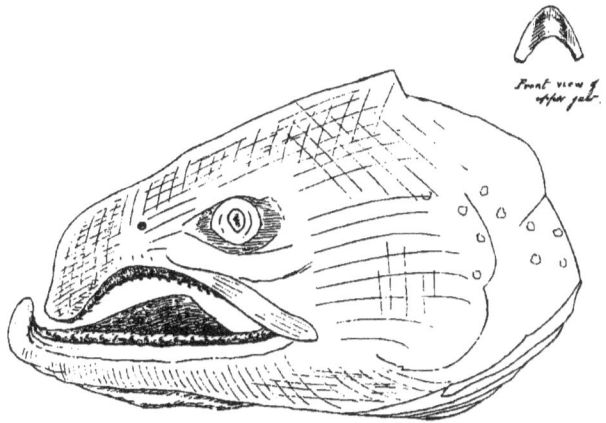

MALFORMED HEAD OF SEA-TROUT, 9 LBS. (½ LIFE-SIZE).

be acceptable, the game should be kept up, as by tomorrow there is no knowing where they may be; and, instead of meeting them in shoals, the angler may very easily pick up but one or two now and again in various pools.

In pools near the tideway these fish may be met

Salmonidæ of Norway. 87

running up with each tide, and, consequently, they are to be found with greater certainty.

The sea-trout of from 10 to 16 lbs. in weight is a remarkably handsome fish, and game to a degree; yet I take it that there are few anglers who would not prefer to kill a salmon of the same size, or even less, and although I am not of the number, there can be little doubt that the flesh of the salmon is more highly esteemed than that of the sea-trout; so, from all points of view, Salmo trutta has to be content with second place.

The sea-trout, like the salmon, seeks the upper pools of rivers, the tributaries, or the lakes for breeding purposes, but within a couple of weeks of his entrance does not so entirely disdain the angler's lure, for I have killed them frequently with the fly in proximity to the borders of lakes, or upon shallow water surrounding islands, etc.

I have fished many small rivers much frequented by sea-trout, but neither in these, nor in the larger ones, have I seen or killed the herling (the grilse of the sea-trout), and I believe that these fish, bred in those rivers, spend their grilse stage of existence in the fjords, or, maybe, even in the sea itself.

The size and natural habits of the sea-trout allows and induces him to penetrate far up into the country, and he may be found at the present day in lakes many miles distant from the fjord, from which connection has been severed by landslips of ages past.

His form and colour, alas! are no more, but the peculiarities incidental to his race yet remain by which his species can be identified, and some history be gleaned of the district he now inhabits.

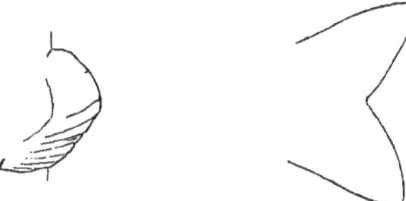

GILL-COVER AND TAIL OF HERLING, ½ LB. (⅓ LIFE-SIZE).

The annexed sketches pertaining to the sea-trout I made from Norwegian fish; but those of the herling I took from a fish caught in the Dumfriesshire Esk.

BULL-TROUT (*Salmo eriox*; Norsk, *Graa ørret*).

Shape.—Head, clumsy and coarse; body, bulky and inelegant.

Scales.—Of the brightness of fresh-cut lead; not lustrous.

Colour.—Back, dark green, shading lighter to white flanks and belly, but of a leaden shade throughout.

Marking.—Freely marked with black spots rather

Salmonidæ of Norway.

square in shape, and without regard to medial line. Some fish have no spots below medial line. Before first visit to sea spotted with black and red marks.

Gill-covers.—Round in outline and irregular, especially in males. Freely spotted.

Teeth.—Upper jaw, two rows.
Under jaw, one row.
Vomer, one row.
Tongue, two rows.

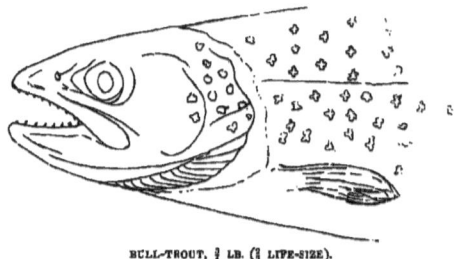

BULL-TROUT, ¾ LB. (¾ LIFE-SIZE).

Fins.—Dorsal, brownish green, blotched with black.
Adipose, slate, tipped with orange.
Pectoral, ventral, anal, before first visit to sea, orange; afterwards, slate-colour to white.

Tail.—When young, roundly forked; square when old; when very old, convex. Colour, dusky slate.

The bull-trout is about the best-abused fish in Norway.

Angling Travels in Norway.

Every hand is against him, and, except by the caterers of hotel or steamboat, and by the lower classes, he is regarded simply as vermin; indeed, by all he is treated as such, and only those above named will either eat his flesh in default of choicer food, or will palm him off upon their guests as sea-trout or "lax."

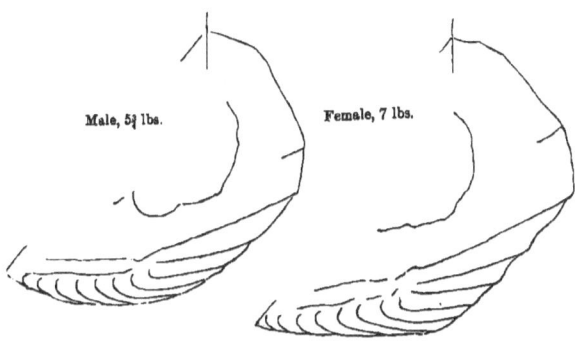

GILL-COVERS (⅔ LIFE-SIZE).

The bull-trout is a glutton, and partakes of all food that comes within his reach, however coarse it may be, but his favourite meal is of the ova of the salmon and sea-trout; and it is on account of his poaching habits in this respect that neither law nor mercy is extended towards him.

It is extremely unfortunate that his nature should lead him into such disgrace, yet in spite of all efforts to

Salmonidæ of Norway.

exterminate him, he flourishes as a green bay-tree, and laughs at his enemies.

His greedy nature causes him to boldly seize the fly or minnow, and then he tries all he knows to shake loose from the hook, and, if his efforts prove unavailing, he makes as stern a fight for life as do the superior species of Salmonidæ.

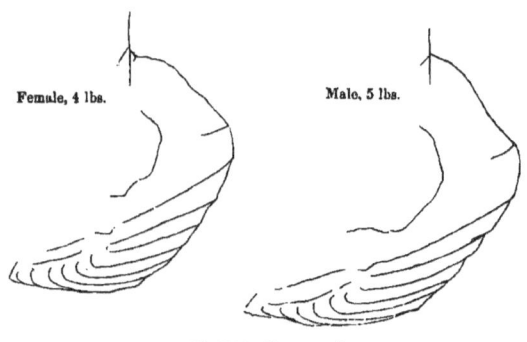

GILL-COVERS (⅔ LIFE-SIZE).

The bull-trout ascends the rivers at about the same time as the sea-trout, or even a little before, and will continue to "run" for some weeks; then those running up the lower waters of the rivers become few and far between; but upon some rivers there is a considerable autumn run, which is more unusual with the Salmonidæ in Norway.

They run up in shoals, and, as the water is clearing off, are encountered in rather shallow heads of gravelly pools.

In such situations the angler may encounter a colony of these fish, and a merry time will be experienced, as a bull-trout of even 4 or 5 lbs. will stream the line from the salmon-reel as he savagely shakes his head in the endeavour to free the hook.

He makes a stubborn fight for a few minutes, and then will in all probability make up stream in slackish water close to the bank, seeming as if settled, yet it is quite possible he may still have a deal of fight left, and may effect escape at the last moment.

It is distasteful to waste valuable time in killing these fish, yet the salmon-angler sacrifices an hour or so with the object of keeping down their numbers.

As the water falls these fish break up the colony and disperse; they then occupy swift-running streams, taking advantage of stones which will afford them even slight shelter.

The larger fish of this species take up their abode in deeper pools, in which they will lie just off the edge of the stream.

Bull-trout may be found in large numbers in thin water just previous to the spawning season, and in some districts the farmers and riparian proprietors destroy large

Salmonidæ of Norway. 93

numbers with staves, treating them as vermin and putting them into the salt-tub. The colour, quality, and greed of the bull-trout are all against him, yet one cannot but feel sorry for the treatment he receives, for he is a game one.

Until the bull-trout first visits the sea he retains his pink spots, and I have killed many in this stage weighing

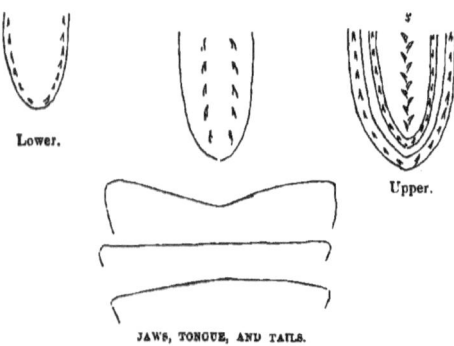

JAWS, TONGUE, AND TAILS.

from ¾ lb. to 1½ lb., and I am of opinion that the instinct which prompts an early visit to the sea is not so strong in his nature as it is in that of the salmon or sea-trout.

I have killed fish of 1 lb. weight, strangers to salt water, and have extracted from them a quarter of a pint of coarse worms, some half digested, others but recently swallowed; and, again, I have cut open a fish of this weight and discovered a like quantity of grass-moths, caked together and sprinkled with the silvery powder of their wings.

I have met with two varieties of the adult bull-trout, both precisely similar in all respects except as to their marking.

The one variety has very few spots below the medial line, and all the spots are rather far apart; the other is more thickly spotted, and the pattern extends a couple of inches or so below the medial line.

The two varieties appeal to the eye at once, that with few markings being the handsomer fish of the two, but they are both bull-trout.

In the adult bull-trout it is frequently impossible to recognize any pink or orange marking at the edge or tip of the adipose fin, but in many cases the colour can be readily distinguished if the fin be allowed to dry.

I have only upon rare occasions met the kelt of these species after the middle of June, so they probably drop down with the break-up of the winter ice.

The annexed drawings of the bull-trout I took from Norwegian fish.

Salmonidæ of Norway.

TROUT (*Salmo fario*; Norsk, *ørret*). (For description, see Map.)

There is scarcely a river, stream, lake, or pond in Norway which may not be said to contain trout differing in average size, colour, and shape in accordance with the characteristics of the watershed and the water they inhabit.

Some of the fast-running salmon rivers which I have

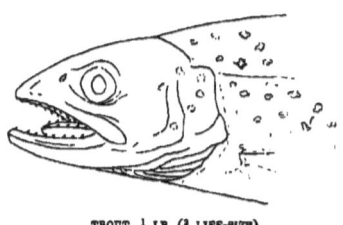

TROUT, ¼ LB. (⅔ LIFE-SIZE).

fished contain few trout, and many small lakes among the hills are said to have sheltered no trout, until a small stock was transferred to them from the nearest river or lake.

In the larger rivers I have observed trout of from 6 lbs. to 8 lbs. in weight feeding at the junction of some backwater with the main stream. These backwaters, as I have previously mentioned, are nurseries for the young of several species of Salmonidæ, and for this reason are

96 Angling Travels in Norway.

frequently selected as abiding places by the Salmo fario of large dimensions.

In these situations he can obtain an unlimited supply of solid food, of which his proportions and condition give evidence; he grows and thickens in much the same style as the Thames trout, and much resembles this fish in

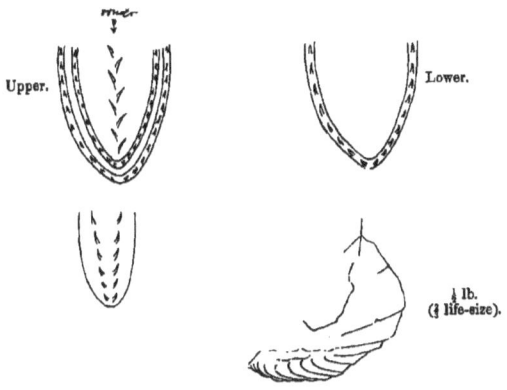

JAWS, TONGUE, AND GILL-COVER.

appearance and in wariness. These large trout, however, appear to require a change of diet, and towards the end of June, or at the beginning of July, will drop down into the main stream to a distance of fifty to one hundred yards in order to partake of winged food, which is more abundantly brought within their reach by the breeze and stream of the river.

While thus engaged they take up positions below

Salmonidæ of Norway.

the roughest portion of the pool, and when they have risen I have frequently been near enough to determine their species.

They are exceedingly wary, and, although I have spent hours in the endeavour to kill them, I have only upon a single occasion succeeded in hooking one, and fortunately killed him, upon an ordinary small March brown. He weighed 7 lbs., and was a very fine fish.

Previous to landing him I was certain of his species, and the peculiar swirl and swish of the trout's rise when feeding is different to that of either salmon, sea-trout, or bull-trout.

Taking them in their order of merit, the next best trout I have killed were those captured in fast-running, gravel-bottomed pools of rivers scarcely one hundred yards above the outlet into the lake.

These fish ranged from 1 lb. to 3 lbs. in weight, and by the middle of July were in splendid condition, both in respect of colour and proportion, in great contrast to those in the rock-bound pools scarce fifty yards above, which were as long as eels and brown as berries.

The fine-conditioned yellow trout I have only killed in such situations as above described; they give excellent sport, but are most disappointing when brought to table, the colour of the flesh being but a yellowish pink, and they cut up none too crisply.

The brown trout I have killed by the hundreds in rivers, and pools of rivers, whose beds have embraced every composition, flooded either by the product of glacier, or spring water mixed with melted snow.

The colouring and condition of these fish will naturally be in accordance with the surroundings. Some are light in colour and round in outline, others are of dusky hue, lank, and apparently ill-fed.

It is said that "beauty is but skin-deep," and these long, dusky trout well illustrate the proverb, for although they appear of such condition that would prompt their return to the water, in reality they are in the perfect stage of their existence. They have conformed to the exigencies of the occasion, and, what is more, have thriven under difficulties. They fight as lions, and when cut open their flesh is of the colour of pink blotting-paper, with a layer of fat between the flakes.

I have killed trout in chains of lakes connected by rivers of small and medium size which are fed for some miles by springs and snow-water, then at a point the melted water of a glacier may augment the stream, and impart to it, for a few miles, that peculiar greenish tint.

Above the influx of the glacier-water the trout have been from $\frac{1}{2}$ lb. to 2 lbs. or more apiece, but in this greenish-coloured water the fish became very scarce, and only weighing about $\frac{1}{4}$ lb. each ; but further down, as the

Salmonidæ of Norway.

water again brightened, the number and size of the trout increased.

Many Norwegian lakes contain the species of lake-trout richly marked with pink spots, each surrounded with a yellow halo or ring. They are much more handsome fish than the other two species above mentioned, and are greater in depth from dorsal fin to the belly. I have killed them chiefly of from 2 lbs. to 4 lbs. in weight. I have it upon the authority of Mr. Fleetwood Sandeman that, in some lakes which we have fished together, this species existed some years ago in much greater numbers, but they appear to have been ousted by other species, which have proportionately increased; with these I shall attempt to deal later on.

The annexed drawings of the trout I took from Norwegian fish.

CHAR (Norsk, *Røie*).

I have killed these fish with fly, spoon and minnow, in lakes and in lake-like expansions of rivers, from ½ lb. to 1½ lbs. in weight.

The following is a description of the fish:—

Body.—The upper two-thirds is grey, shaded darker from the medial line up to the root of the dorsal fin, and spotted with white.

The lowest one-third portion of the body, including the belly, is coloured a bright orange-red.

The medial line appears as if formed of a series of stitches running diagonally but parallel to each other.

Gill-covers.—Almost free of indentations, and in outline a perfect oval.

Fins.—Dorsal : Dark grey.
        Adipose : Grey, faintly tinged with orange
        Pectoral : Orange to red.
        Ventral and anal : Bright red, lowest rays pure white.
        Caudal : Dark orange.

Teeth.—Upper jaw : two rows.
        Lower jaw : one row.
        Tongue : two rows.

The char is a most elegantly-shaped fish from nose to tail points.

SEA-CHAR (Norsk, *Sø-røie*).

These fish are found in the rivers and lakes of Nordland and further north ; they run up to 3 lbs. and 4 lbs., and are handsome sporting fish. When recently from the sea their sides are of a light orange pink, which grows more brilliant with their sojourn in fresh water. They spawn in the lakes or deep pools, and will feed even under a brilliant sun.

Salmonidæ of Norway.

In other respects the description of this fish is the same as that of the Char.

GRAYLING (*Salmo thymallus*).

The fish are found in Norway, but are more plentiful in Sweden. I have never gone out with the special purpose of killing them, but those I have killed are of the ordinary description as found in Great Britain, with no especial peculiarities. They run from 1 lb. to 3 lbs., and even more, in weight.

CHAPTER XI.

TO DISTINGUISH BETWEEN TROUT AND SMOLT.

I HAVE heard anglers of experience declare a fish of the Salmo species to be a sea-trout, because they were nearly certain that he was neither a salmon nor a bull-trout, and although the said anglers had fished for nearly a score of years, neither of them could name the characteristic points of the fish.

When such lack of knowledge exists among matured anglers, it is no wonder that the trout-fisher, unaccustomed to salmon rivers, should experience difficulty in distinguishing between small trout and smolt, and as this disability may possibly lead to trouble, as well as being the cause of the destruction of immature fish, it is advisable that he be acquainted with the characteristics of both species.

Most of us can recall instances of our own hesitation in the expression of a definite opinion upon the subject, and probably few of us at one time or another have not unintentionally retained smolts, until practice and the application of the several tests have enabled us to determine the species at a glance.

A difficulty we have to contend with in the identification of Salmonidæ lies in the fact that those of a kind vary one from another, and the task becomes more arduous when it so happens that the variations in two specimens of different species tend in the direction of each other's normal characteristics. For instance, if a trout be light in colour, and the finger-marks on the sides of the smolt happen to be very indistinct, the result is an unusual resemblance between the two.

It should be understood that, although the following characteristics are generally correct, instances are of common occurrence in which fish do not clearly illustrate some *one or more* of them—in which case the further tests must be applied until the question is decided.

To the trained eye a considerable difference exists between the shape and outline of trout and smolt, for while that of the latter is elegance itself, the trout is of more clumsy build, particularly as regards the head, jaw, and gill-cover, and his outline is more or less lumpy.

When frequenting streams running fast over gravelly beds, the trout may be as bright in colour as the smolt, especially early in the season, just prior to the smolt migration, for he is not as yet, so to say, in full plumage.

Again, the experienced angler will generally recognize the smolt as soon as hooked by the continuous wriggles made in the effort to escape, whereas under like predicament the trout's resistance is more staid and stubborn.

One word of caution—When about to fish a salmon-river for trout, the novice is generally informed that he can readily distinguish between them and smolts by the bars or finger-marks which run across the sides of the latter, by which in many districts they have acquired the name of "brandling."

This, however, is by no means a sure test, as young trout frequently retain these bars, although not of such vivid colour as in the smolt. On the other hand, the bars upon a well-grown smolt may have become so indistinct that they do not catch the eye until viewed in a certain light, and this is more especially the case with the smolt which has existed for two years in the parr stage.

The more certain characteristics of the two species are :—

In *Trout*, the spots are distributed over the flanks without regard to the medial line.

In *Smolt*, there are few, if any, spots on the body

below the medial line, with the exception of a few immediately behind the gill-covers.

In *Smolt*, the gill-covers are spotted without regard to the medial line on the body.

In *Trout*, the adipose fin is marked at the tip with a spot ranging from orange to pink.

In *Smolt*, the adipose fin is of slate colour and unspotted.

In *Trout*, the dorsal fin is spotted or blotched.

In *Smolt*, the dorsal fin is plain colour.

In *Trout*, the lowest ray of the anal fin is marked with a *white line*.

In *Smolt*, there is no white line.

In *Trout*, the pectoral and ventral fins are of orange colour, and brightest at the tips.

In *Smolt*, the pectoral and ventral fins are yellowish in colour.

In *Trout*, the outline of the gill-cover is angular and irregular.

In *Smolt*, the outline of the gill-cover is oval and regular.

In *Trout*, the scales are firmly attached.

In *Smolt*, the scales are easily detached, and will come off in handling.

CHAPTER XII.

TACKLE FOR NORWAY.

THE angler who is accustomed to fish the large rivers of Scotland and England would not find much amiss with his tackle for use in Norway, but, as will have been gathered from the previous chapters, Norwegian rivers have their peculiarities, and consequently suitable tackle should be selected.

Anglers have their own ideas and preferences as regards tackle, and it is here unnecessary to argue upon the subject, so I will only describe the shape and make of the articles which have given satisfactory results, leaving the individual to modify in accordance with his personal ideas and comfort.

Wading-trousers and their attendant gear should be provided, for although the particular river which a man goes out to fish may not require them, he may meet with invitations to fish elsewhere, or may take a higher beat of his own river, and if he have them he is independent.

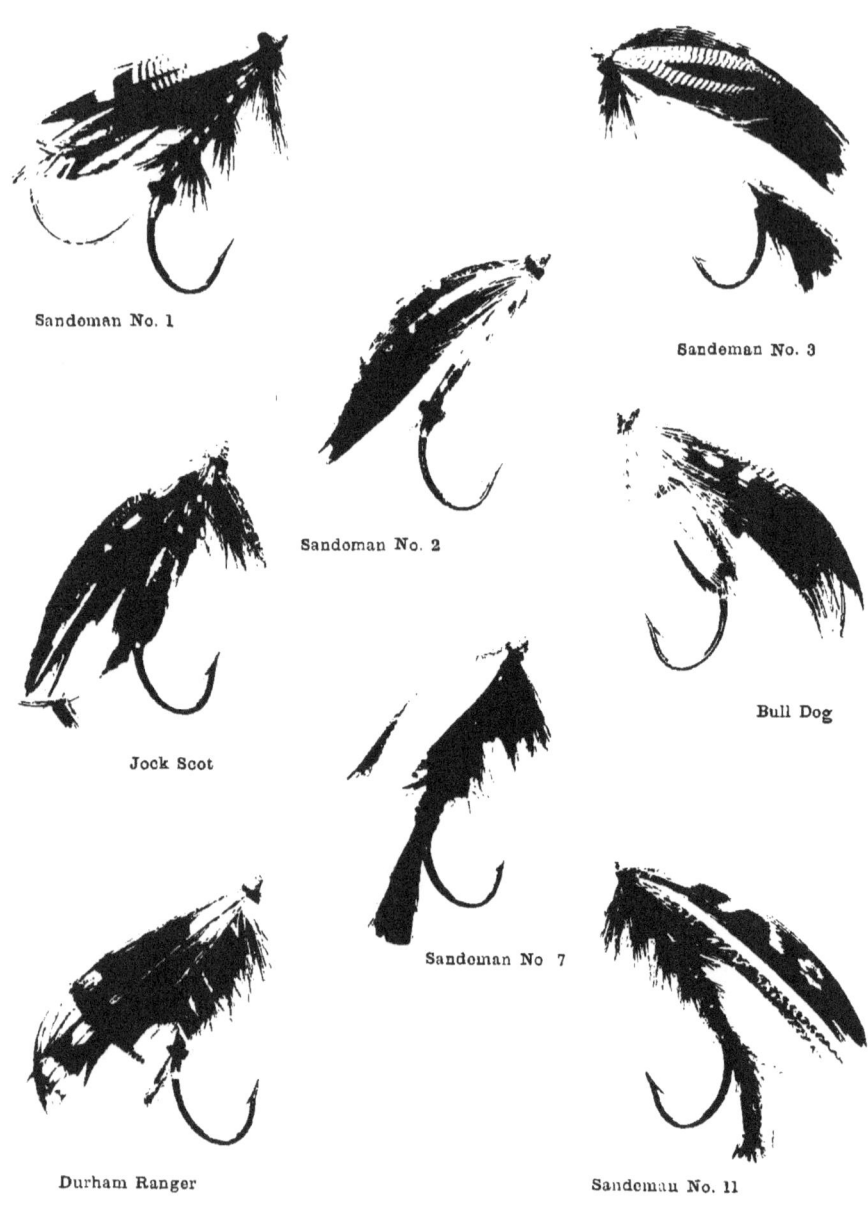

For Patterns vide Appendix.

LLANOVER

Mintern Bros lith

Tackle for Norway.

A stout waterproof coat, reaching down to the ankles, should be included in the kit, for the rain often comes down incessantly, or in very heavy showers, and in this mountainous country, where the drops fall as large as a sixpence, one can be wetted through within ten minutes. India-rubber waterproofs are lighter than oilskins, but they are not so serviceable, as they tear more easily. I prefer oilskins for rough work, and one can use them as tarpaulins upon occasion without harming them.

Perhaps the best system of waterproof clothing, especially for boat-work, is a skirt to buckle round the waist, and to reach down to the ankle, and a coat to reach down to the knees, the whole surmounted with a sou'-wester, or felt hat sufficiently wide of brim when turned down to conduct the wet clear of the coat-collar; and the coat comes in handy for use with waders.

Even during the summer months all descriptions of weather may be encountered in Norway, and it would be most unwise not to include in the kit warm winter-clothing.

The valleys are frequently confined by ranges of hills or mountains several thousand feet high, and whatever may be the direction of the wind aloft, its influence is such that upon the level of the river the current of

108   Angling Travels in Norway.

air travels directly either up or down stream; in point of fact, one exists in a perpetual draught.

Thus, should the wind veer a few points aloft, it is

OLE AND J.

possible that in the valley it may chop completely round, and incidentally cause a trying change of temperature. In the forenoon, the breeze wafted from one direction may

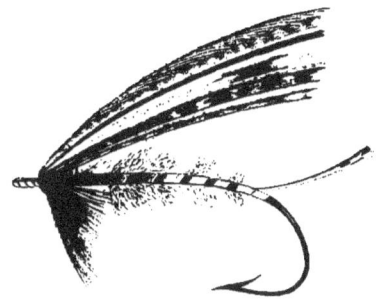

BRANSTY.

Minturn Bros lith.

Tackle for Norway.

be soft and balmy, then, with little warning, it may chop round and bring an icy blast from snow-covered mountains, a change unwelcome and even dangerous. The natives well appreciate the sudden changes of climate, and rarely are unprovided with warm neck and chest clothing while engaged in fishing—or even while following ordinary occupations. This steady and continuous draught is far more trying than an ordinary open breeze, and whether it course up or down stream, opposes with much force the angler's line, and a powerful rod is absolutely necessary to make a good cast.

The Rod.—The question of the make, length, and weight of the rod in fly-fishing for salmon must be left to the taste of the angler, who should best know his own capabilities. He generally thinks he knows his own abilities, but in my humble opinion he frequently underrates them.

For the purpose of illustration, my height is 5 feet $9\frac{1}{2}$ inches, and weight 11 stone, and I use a 20-ft. Castleconnell all day long without the slightest inconvenience. I am inclined to think that it is not so much the rod that tires the angler as the want of knowledge and method of wielding it.

Many anglers want to do all the work themselves, whereas I am sure that if they would only give the rod a chance we should hear less of those *heavy* 18-ft. rods, etc.

For fishing small rivers and for boat-work, an 18-ft. rod may answer the purpose, and it may be argued that a certain make of rod of this length can cast as long a line as may be required. Well and good, perhaps it can—but that is only half of the story. In the first place, for *continuous* long casting, I prefer to cast easily with a 20-ft. than cast at the top of my form with an 18-ft.; and, in the second place, it should be noted that the longer rod enables the angler to hang the fly better over his fish, and this is no mean consideration in fishing rapid rivers, where the bait is swept quickly away; and, thirdly, a big rod gives more control over fish in heavy water, although the cast terminate with a yard of single-gut.

For harling and casting from the reel, a 15-ft. rod is a good weapon, and handy in the boat. I use a rod for these purposes composed of lower joints of male bamboo cane and the top of greenheart. For casting from the reel a stiff rod is requisite, and this serves well for harling, as the top does not swing about, but keeps the bait steady in the water, which to my mind is advantageous, as the boat gives plenty of motion.

The Reel should be of 5 inches diameter, and contain 100 yards of dressed line, and beneath it 50 yards of backing, while for fishing such rivers as the Tana, the line should be 200 yards in all.

SAGHOUG.

Mintern Bros. lith.

Tackle for Norway.

I use salmon reels, with check of double strength, which requires special construction; but the mechanism is simple. Messrs. Hardy Brothers make them for me, and I find that the extra power is of great importance in any description of salmon angling.

For sea-trout, the rod as used in Great Britain serves well, and for trout fishing, a 12-ft. fly-rod and 10-ft. trolling-rod will be handy, with reels and lines to match them.

Casts.—For salmon, will be required of treble-gut throughout, and others, of two yards treble and one yard single, and sometimes even three yards of single-gut. For sea-trout and trout, single-gut casts are best.

Treble and single gut traces should be provided for harling and trolling (fitted, of course, with swivels), or steel wire traces in their place.

I always use casts composed of two yards treble and one yard single gut, with No. 5/0 flies and under, while for No. 6/0, and above, I use treble-gut casts—not on account of the fish or water, but only on account of the weight of the fly, for I think the best single-gut is practically as strong as the ordinary treble; but a heavy fly, especially if it be dressed on an eyed-hook, is apt to *neck* the extremity of the cast.

Flies.—My experience is that Norwegian salmon are very free takers, and I do not find that they are very particular as to flies; most of the usual standard patterns kill well, such as the Jock Scott, Durham Ranger, Popham, Black-Dose, Black Doctor, Silver Doctor, Silver Grey, and the Llanover, of which, by-the-by, there are several dressings, but I usually fish with my own patterns, as given in "By Hook and by Crook,"* and I have no reason to change. The sizes should be from No. 7/0 to No. 2/0. For sea-trout, the ordinary patterns suffice, and the same dressed upon smaller hooks are better for trout than our English trout-flies, which are too plain in colour, and too small in size.

Red-bodied flies, with tinsel rib, and black body with tinsel, are about the best killers, and a bit of red in the tail is a distinct advantage.

Baits.—For salmon, spoons, 3 inches to 1 inch, both heavy and light. Phantoms, blue, brown, and silver; 4 inches to 2 inches. Devons, the same sizes.

Prawns and tackle are useful, as salmon and grilse will take them and nothing else at times, especially in low water; and I find that the "Sandeman Prawn Tackle" rarely misses; in fact, it was my Norwegian experiences which perfected it.

For sea-trout, bull-trout, and trout, smaller baits of the

* The best dressings of my patterns of Salmon Flies are obtainable of F. M. Walbran, New Station Street, Leeds, who keeps several sizes in stock.

GŬLA.

Mintern Bros. lith.

Tackle for Norway.

above varieties are requisite; and I have found the 2-in. silver phantom a real good killer in lakes, and the older he was the better he killed.

Leads of different weights are necessary in harling, and those with wires like corkscrews at either end are the easiest to change.

Intelligent leading contributes to success, and I always like to get well *down* to my fish.

It is not possible to purchase reliable tackle in Norway, so the angler should be well provided, as also with spare rings and materials for tackle mending, including wax, varnish, silk, flax thread, hooks, triangles, split-rings, etc.

The annexed sketches are of flies which I have proved to be excellent killers, assisted by *the very best* single or treble gut.

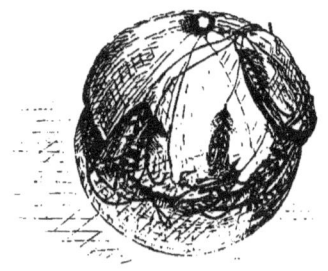

ALL SIXES AND SEVENS.

CHAPTER XIII.

HARLING AND BOAT-ANGLING.

HARLING and angling from a boat are generally regarded as inferior classes of sport, as compared to bank or wading-fishing, yet they are the only practical methods by which certain pools, or even some entire rivers, can be fished, barring the use of the otter ; and they provide many with the means of sport who, either by physical disability or by advanced age, are unequal to the exertion of a day's bank angling.

I am not certain that those of us who can wield with ease an 18-ft. or 20-ft. rod do not now and again welcome a harling pool, especially when fishing a river which entails continued long casting ; but no matter what comparative value we attach to harling, of a certainty it is no fool's work, and, like all other branches of angling, it must be conducted with intelligence and system, consequently the art possesses many details demanding consideration.

Harling and Boat-angling.

In casting from the bank or bed of a river, the angler can make certain of covering every foot of water within his reach; but not so the harler, unless he and his companion on the thwart be workmen of the first class.

Angling in combination, which boat-work affords, can only be enjoyed in the same degree by oarsman and angler if they both be equally good, or equally bad, at their work; and I would rather not fish than be obliged to contend with the vagaries of an incompetent oarsman, while I must confess that it is no treat to row for a bad angler.

A good oarsman gets sick of working for a bad or inattentive angler, just as a good dog wearies of working for a bad shot. Neither man nor dog can compensate for the shortcomings of his companion.

In boat-fishing, be it casting or harling, the oarsman's work is of every bit as great importance, and requires as much skill, as that of the angler, and I would as soon row the boat as fish—or, perhaps, I should say, hold the rod, for, indeed, the oarsman is as much fishing as the man who grasps the rod.

No episode in angling gives one more pleasure than when, rowing the boat, a fish takes the angler's fly at the exact spot which one has previously indicated as a "smittle shop." Such happy result does not happen as frequently as could be desired; yet, when it does, great is the reward.

I propose to divide my remarks upon harling under two heads—" Rowing the Boat " and " Angling," and will, in the first place, venture a few hints upon the former.

HARLING—ROWING THE BOAT.

In harling, as in all other modes of angling, it is of primary importance to cover the water systematically; and in the first place, the boat should be rowed sufficiently high up the pool to allow the flies or baits to be arranged in working order some few yards above the lie of the fish; then it should be rowed across from bank to bank, dropping down a yard or so at each beat, until the pool ends.

It is a very common fault with oarsmen to harl a pool too quickly, or to take too much new water in at each beat; but, when it is possible to hold the boat, no more than four to five feet should intervene between each drift; and, to make certain of this, the oarsman should keep his eye on some landmark of either stone, tree, or projection upon the bank, as, after having fished a pool, it is most unsatisfactory to feel that half the water has been missed.

To row a boat for harling or casting, the oarsman must be continually " at her," no matter how slow the pace of the stream. It is impossible to keep a boat steady if any length of time be allowed between the strokes, as in that case she is certain to " run off," and the operation of putting her straight entirely upsets steady angling. To "keep dipping" is the maxim.

The angle at which the boat is held against the stream is also of great importance.

It is obvious that the craft offers the least resistance when heading straight up stream; and it follows that if she be held at an angle against it, increased power will be requisite to hold her up; and the speed at which she travels from bank to bank will be much increased, in all probability to the detriment of good angling.

I have frequently found myself flying across the river for no earthly reason than my boatman's ignorance, and my patience has been well-nigh exhausted in the endeavour to induce him to take it more quietly, and I have found a period of some days necessary to break him thoroughly of the habit, as, unconsciously, he will now and again revert to his former style.

There are, doubtless, many good native boatmen, but, as far as my experience goes, the majority of them are indifferent performers, and some are very bad, although not worse than many I have had to contend with in Great Britain, and as the knowledge of angling matters which Norwegian boatmen possess has been acquired from British sportsmen and *others*, their incapacity in a measure reflects upon ourselves.

The handling of a pleasure-boat is far from being a

matter of general knowledge, and the art of working a craft for angling purposes is still more rarely practised.

It is of but little use to complain of a man's rowing unless one can give a practical demonstration, as otherwise he is apt to argue with himself, " I should like to see him do it better."

It is uninteresting work to harl a pool which affords little cover, and, in consequence, the fish may lie anywhere; it is much better sport when the bed contains well-defined resting-places for fish, and in such situations the expert oarsman can display his ability and knowledge of the water. It is a treat to watch a man so work his boat that the lure swings temptingly across each well-known shelter with as much precision as if the catch were being fished from the bank. Such fine art in harling can only be appreciated by one who knows the water, and who, like the oarsman, has killed fish in it.

The pace at which I have been raced across from side to side has compelled me to imagine that my boatman was of opinion that the salmon delights to rush after his food; but that he was not in reality of this belief I have afterwards ascertained; he was merely acting by force of thoughtless habit. I prefer to harl quite slowly, and only to quicken pace should the shallowness of the pool oblige me to do so, in order to keep the bait from fouling the river-bed; but moderation should be observed, for

Harling and Boat-angling. 119

inasmuch as in a given stream the lateral exposure of the bait will be about equal to that of the boat, it follows that a wider expanse of bait will be exhibited to the fish when the boat travels fast across the river. But this fact does not enter largely into my calculations, as I take other precautions to bring the lure well within their range of vision.

FIVE MINUTES' REST.

Until he is broken of the habit, the boatman delights in running the craft hard aground, especially if one has a fish on, and one's back is turned shorewards; he does this from thoughtlessness, and not with the intention of shooting one into the bottom of the boat, yet the system has no merit. I have fished with some men who would have been first-class in a boat had they possessed the gift to appreciate the "set" of the stream, but somehow or another they have not had it in them, and, although one may have repeatedly instructed them how to head the boat, they never grasp the situation. A really good boatman must be a good oarsman, a good waterman, an intelligent observer of the habits of fish and the water they inhabit, and he must be fond of the sport. It is somewhat rare to find such a combination in an individual, thus first-class boatmen are scarce.

HARLING—ANGLING.

In the first part of this chapter I have endeavoured to describe the difficulties with which the rower of the boat has to contend, and it is essential that the angler should assist him by good and systematic work, otherwise the skill of the oarsman will avail little or nothing.

The angler, in the first place, decides upon the number of rods he intends to employ, and then rigs them out with lines, casts, baits, etc.; the oarsman next rows him to the neck of the pool, and holds the boat until the baits are let out to the desired length.

The pace of the stream, the depth of water, and the weight of the bait are the three factors which determine the length of line to be fished when harling, and it is of the greatest importance that this length should not, without good reason, be increased when fishing a pool, to avoid the possibility of missing even a yard of water.

If the lines be maintained at one length, the oarsman, if proficient, can cover the pool foot by foot, but when they are continually being altered this is almost an impossibility.

When a man whom I am rowing frequently alters the length of his line in casting or in harling it disgusts me with the business, and if unaware that his procedure resulted from ignorance or want of thought, I would row straight ashore; hence, when the rod-work falls to my share, I behave to my oarsman as I would have him behave to me.

The angler himself is perhaps the best judge of the number of rods he can employ at one time when harling. Personally, I use two in fishing a medium-sized pool, and three in larger waters. When using three rods at a time, the usual plan is to put one out pointing astern, and the remaining two, one at each side of the boat, which are kept steady in notches cut for the purpose in the edge of the counter.

Some anglers place a weight upon the line at the bottom of the boat, which strikes the fish upon seizing the bait; others trust to the check of the reel; but I prefer to make certain of driving the hooks home, and for the purpose have a rail about two feet in length, fastened to the flooring-boards of the boat, with space between it and the flooring to admit the butt of the rod.

I then place the rod at the desired angle (about 45°), resting in the notch in the counter, and the butt under the rail, and turn the reel over until the handle is in contact with the flooring.

I now thrust the butt further under the rail, at the same time maintaining the reel in position, until the rod is jambed fast enough to keep steady, and by this adjustment I accurately determine with what force the fish will strike himself.

I always adopt this system with reels having checks of ordinary strength, and have never met with disaster by breakage, while the fish are generally well hooked, but I admit the necessity of some little delicacy in the manipulation, and of late I have had my reels made with double strength of check, which is by itself sufficient to strike a fish.

When harling with a Nottingham reel, it will be found more convenient to fix the rod in the position described above, with the revolving side itself against the flooring, as the handles are generally too short and set too near the centre of the reel to be serviceable for this purpose.

To avoid counting the number of yards of line to be released from the reel at each harl, I attach a piece of waxed silk to each line at about twenty-five yards from

Harling and Boat-angling.

the extremity, and cut off the ends, so that about an inch remains; this saves a deal of time and trouble, and is more precise than guess-work.

When harling with three rods, I usually let out a different length of line from each—say rod No. 1—25 yards, rod No. 2—26 yards, and rod No. 3—27 yards. Thus, at each beat, the baits, if hanging straight down stream, would enclose six feet of water, but, by the lateral course of the boat, the distance between the first and last bait is reduced.

If the boat be well rowed, every fish will be at least twice covered by this system, and if the oarsman be less expert, he will be more unlikely to miss water than if the lines were all of a length.

It is no certainty that a fish catches sight of every bait which passes more or less near his head, and, again, a fish does not necessarily go for each bait he sees, so it is well to afford him every opportunity.

Fish often rest at the very tail of a pool, right on the head of the next, so it is advisable not to reel up before the very last moment. I have killed many fish by the observance of this practice.

It may be said that, as a general rule, the Norsk boatman rows a boat for angling in the manner he has been taught by British anglers, and, upon the whole, does fairly well; yet many of us like to fish in our own ways, and must, accordingly, instruct our companions on the thwart.

A common fault with rowers is to let the boat slip down too fast, and to obviate this it is, in the first place, essential that the weight, size, and construction of the craft be suitable for the work in hand; then the boatman must sit down to his task, and if one-man power be not sufficient, two hands must be employed; but the boat *must* be held up so that the pool can be fished literally foot by foot.

It is a very general habit among boatmen when harling to switch the craft sharply round when turning near the bank to commence the next beat.

This procedure is suggested partly by anxiety to keep the bait clear of the bottom, and in slow-running pools it has advantages; but, unless when absolutely necessary, I much prefer to have the boat held up before the turn, so that the bait may hang straight down stream before the next beat be commenced, as by this means the line is first upon a curve, then it hangs straight, and then becomes again curved in the opposite direction, whereas, if the boat be switched sharply round, the line for a considerable period is in the form of a semi-circle, or, in other words, greatly bagged, a situation always to be avoided in angling.

When rowing the boat for an angler casting a pool,

Harling and Boat-angling.

the oarsman, in addition to taking his bearings from objects upon the banks, in order to regulate the speed of his descent, should gauge his lateral position in the stream by breaks and sets upon the surface, or by projections or landmarks lower down, and this portion of his work requires strict attention, so that water may not be scamped over, or even entirely missed.

When a fish is hooked while harling with more than one rod, it is not uncommon to row the boat immediately to shore and allow the baits remaining free to fall upon the river's bed until the boatman can reel them up; but to reel up the temporarily unemployed lines previous to running the boat to land is a more sporting procedure, and is in itself a pretty phase of angling. This system may cause a slight delay, but I object to my lines and baits being on the bottom, and take little pleasure in killing fish in careless or flukey fashion.

When harler and angler fish well and systematically together they will not miss many fish; otherwise, it is but mere chance that they effect captures.

When harling with two rods, one displaying a fly and the other a spoon or minnow, I generally hold the fly rod in my hands, in the ordinary manner, and the second rod, showing spoon or minnow, I lay down in the boat upon the opposite side, or I lay the rod down and pull from the reel about a yard of line, which I hold

126 Angling Travels in Norway.

in the fingers of the hand which grasps the fly rod at or below its reel.

The moment I feel a fish take the minnow or spoon, I draw the line smartly back and strike hard, and whether the fish be on or off, I have the satisfaction of knowing that I have done my best to drive the hooks home. When fishing with compound tackle, for a change, I occasionally adopt another system—a very simple one. I lay the two rods down in the bottom of the boat, pointing in different directions, and I hold a line in each hand, and strike hard as soon as I feel a touch.

I have been told that this system is more dangerous to the hands than to the fish, but I have not found it so, for I notice that a salmon, upon being hooked, requires about a second to appreciate the situation, which affords the angler ample time to grasp the rod, but if the angler be not very "quick on his fish," he may lose this second, and perhaps had better not practise this system.

The baits should be carefully laid upon the water, and not thrown in anyhow, for obvious reasons.

"I THINK WE'VE MET BEFORE, DOCTOR."

CHAPTER XIV.

UPON RENTING AND LETTING SALMON RIVERS.

LETTERS appear from time to time in the public press from anglers who, for some reason or another, are dissatisfied with the sport they have obtained as lessees or sub-lessees of Norwegian salmon rivers, and who convey the idea that they have been misled from the outset as to the worth of the fishery, and have in consequence been induced to pay far too high a rent. Under these circumstances the lessor or sub-lessor, if he be a Norwegian, is generally styled an "agent," or a "middleman," with whom, in future transactions, the complainant advises the angling public to deal with extreme caution, and generally concludes with some well-intended advice of more or less value.

It is somewhat interesting to note that, when negotiating for the fishery, the angler was pleased to avail himself of the services of the so-called "agent" or "middleman," so it is to be presumed that at that time he saw nothing reprehensible in the practice of speculation in fisheries, or surely he would not have encouraged it, even to the extent of a single year's rent; but, at the termination of his tenancy, he suddenly discovers that the renting of angling water for gain is a practice to be severely condemned.

That there are plenty of British subjects at the present moment, as regards fisheries, in precisely the same situation as the Norwegian "middleman" is a fact that appears to be conveniently ignored, nor are the terms "agent" and "middleman" applied to them.

It is of little consequence whether the renting of fisheries for the purpose of making a profit in some form or another be approved or decried, for wherever there be a subject for speculation, there will always be some ready to enter the lists. Some profess to distinguish a vast difference between speculation in a fishery and in other sporting, or non-sporting, properties, but I confess that the distinction is too subtle for my understanding, and I see no reason why angling water should be placed upon a sacred pedestal.

In the majority of cases the angling tenant, be he a British or Norwegian subject, in the first instance rents a river with the purpose of fishing it himself during at least some portion of the season; then the question arises, what shall he do with it for the remainder?

Renting and Letting Salmon Rivers. 129

1. Shall he debit himself with a fair proportion of the rent and charge his sub-tenant with the balance?

2. Shall he charge his sub-tenant such a sum as will partially or entirely relieve him of rent during his selected portion of the season?

3. Shall he charge his sub-tenant such a sum as will give him his own portion of the season free of rent, and, over and above that, return a profit?

4. Or, in the event of his sub-letting the fishery for the entire season, shall he be content to get back his rent, or think proper to ask a sum which will show a profit?

I maintain that the pursuit of either course of procedure is the business of the lessor or sub-lessor alone, who surely has the right to fix the value of his property.

Notwithstanding the decline in the intrinsic value of Norwegian fisheries, no doubt there are in existence at the present time many leases at rents under their present market value, having yet a considerable term to run, so it is possible for the holders to make a profit in sub-letting, without charging above what is generally considered a fair price in these days.

On the other hand, the farmers have asked and obtained such rents for leases of more recent date that a profit cannot be obtained in sub-letting unless a price be asked in excess of what competent anglers would consider to be their value.

Now the question arises, What is the value of a fishery? An extremely difficult one to answer, for it contains so many factors. It is all very well to argue that a moor is worth no more than a certain sum per head of each grouse killed, or that the rent of a salmon river shall not exceed the equivalent of a fixed sum for each fish landed; but of what practical use are either of these limits so long as there are men in the world who will exceed them, and whose incomes enable them to attach a comparatively small value to the coin of the realm.

It simply amounts to this: that the market value of a fishery, like that of most commodities, is precisely what it will fetch, and, however galling it may be, we poorer brethren must for the time being succumb, directly or indirectly, to those whose while it is worth to outbid us; and, unfortunately for us, there can be but little doubt that angling rents, both at home and abroad, are steadily on the rise, for the rank and file of the noble army of anglers is being daily recruited.

The Anglo-Norwegian angler, who at one time had Norsk rivers almost entirely to himself, has many competitors, and can we be surprised that a professional or business man, who has but one leisure month of twelve,

Renting and Letting Salmon Rivers. 131

should seek the country which will give him the greatest certainty to enjoy his favourite sport? And should we be surprised that he is prepared to pay highly for it? Or should we be surprised when So-and-So, of —— Square, secures a fishery at twice its worth? For does not his name, with "his river in Norway," appear in the columns of the Society newspapers?

Sympathy may be readily extended to the pioneers of angling in Norway who, when wishing to renew their leases, find that they are asked a large increase of rent, but it does not often occur to them to take into account that, for a considerable portion of the expired term, they have enjoyed their sport at a cheap rate. They have a much more genuine grievance should they discover, at the termination of their tenancy, that a new lease has been granted over their heads, and that they must give way to a new lessee, without the option of a renewal.

In these cases there appears to be a tendency on the part of the outgoing tenant to attribute the entire blame of his discomfiture to the new lessee, whom he generally accuses of having gone behind his back; but, on the other hand, it may appear somewhat foolish to rely upon the non-interference of strangers for the continuation of a sporting lease.

The "old Anglo-Norsk hand" is no fool, and I venture to suggest that it is not through inadvertence that he postpones the question of renewal until sometimes too late, but rather does he procrastinate in order to avoid raising the rent against himself by the exhibition of anxiety upon the subject.

I am not certain that the farmers always nurture a superfluity of goodwill towards these lessees, who for a number of years past have had much the best of the bargain, and who, upon low rents, have been netting considerable profits, either in hard cash or in free fishing for themselves. But, be this as it may, I think a man forestalled in a renewal of his lease should blame himself and the lessor quite as much as the incoming tenant.

It is the custom of British anglers not to interfere or compete with one another in sporting rights in Norway, and the same feeling generally exists amongst Norwegians *inter se*, but I doubt if the British exercise the same consideration towards Norwegians, and I know of instances in which they have behaved in precisely the manner that they object to, if adopted by natives of Norway.

I also know of instances in which Norwegians have attempted to undermine the good feeling which existed, or the British tenant imagined to have existed, between himself and riparian proprietors, sometimes with, and sometimes without, success; but whatever opinion we may entertain of this conduct, it is perhaps but fair to bear in mind that the Norwegian strives to obtain the fisheries of his native land, to which he may not unreasonably consider he has a prior claim.

Long after British anglers have thrown up a river, on account of the indifferent sport it afforded, I have known Norwegians step in and take a lease, and for several years exercise considerable self-denial in only lightly fishing it, in order to increase the supply of fish, which is a proof that they can, and do, act unselfishly and as sportsmen.

I have no desire to paint the Norwegian sub-lessor in other than true colours, but I am of opinion that he frequently performs a very useful office, and it is no unusual occurrence for a British angler to sub-lease a river from some one of them for several years in succession.

I have explained in another chapter how the quantity of winter snow lying around the watershed of a river determines the initial prospects of an angling season; and I have known British lessors to have sublet their rivers, rather than fish themselves, when the outlook has been indifferent. In such a case, the sub-lessor knows, or thinks he knows, more than the general public, and there may exist a code of honour, which would condemn such conduct.

In the foregoing lines I have attempted to fairly discuss some of the considerations which arise in the letting and sub-letting of Norwegian rivers, and to describe a few of the difficulties which beset the paths of lessor and lessee.

It goes without saying that it is easier to ascertain particulars of a fishing at home than of one abroad, for the values of British angling rivers are almost public property, whereas those of Scandinavian fisheries are but known to the sportsmen who for some years past have been in the habit of visiting the country, and many of these, for obvious reasons, prefer to exercise a discreet silence.

The number of rivers which in an average year afford good or fair sport is comparatively small, and they are mostly leased to British anglers, who find small difficulty in sub-letting them to members of their acquaintance when so disposed; and these may obtain information as to the prospects of sport; but, fortunately for the general angling public, there are rivers to let every year; but I think that, when dealing with strangers, an angler might avail himself of the assistance of the sporting journals more frequently than appears to be the case, as I think an inquiry would generally be followed by valuable information. In taking a river there are many points to consider :—

The rent you wish to pay.

The length of water and number of pools required.

Renting and Letting Salmon Rivers.

The date and period you wish to fish.
Whether you require harling or fly-casting.
Whether fishing from boat or bank.
The house accommodation.
The distance from England.
The distance of the river from a market for your fish.
The average year's sport.
The average weight of the fish.

And if an angler can satisfy his desires in all these particulars, he is extremely fortunate.

Of these ten questions the lessor and lessee together should be able to supply answers to the first eight, but the two last present greater difficulties, because so few anglers keep a record of fish killed and fish lost. The game-book affords interesting reminiscences and food for reflection, and if a man be fishing by himself there can be no objection to the keeping of it, but when two or more are fishing in company, perhaps it is advisable to dispense with a record of success and failure, for the daily scores are apt to lead to comparison and competition, both of which, to my mind, are detestable in sport.

The contents of a game-book are generally placed at the disposal of a prospective lessee or sub-lessee, but they are of comparatively little value unless details of the season and weather, together with the proficiencies of the rods, be added; otherwise, an inferior angler may be much disappointed should he take a river from the record of a first-class rod; and, again, a first-class fisherman may be deterred by the diary of a bad angler from taking a fishery which, in an average year, would afford him good sport. Thus a game-book may require many notes and explanations in order to provide a trustworthy guide to a fishery.

Many of us anglers do not recognize the fact that we are bad performers, and perhaps it would be more instructive to keep a note of fish lost than one of fish killed; and I strongly advise indifferent anglers not to take expensive fishings, unless they be fully prepared to encounter disappointment. Norwegian salmon are very free takers, and are also very free fighters.

CHAPTER XV.

PRAWN-FISHING FOR SALMON.

No matter in what esteem prawn-fishing may be held as compared with fly and minnow fishing, it is certain that fish are often killed by the prawn when all other lures fail to attract. Some anglers refuse to employ either minnow or prawn, because they will not, or because they know not how to use them, and in consequence miss a deal of what others consider sport.

I confess that, to my mind, the unprejudiced individual who does not handicap himself, but practises the various methods of salmon-angling which provide him with sport in their right times and seasons, has much the best of the argument, and is a better fisherman than he who can only kill fish when the water is in perfect order. In fact, the wisdom of persevering with a lure which for the time being is practically useless does not appeal to me, when a more taking device is at hand, and can be employed without injury to those who may entertain contrary opinions.

138 Angling Travels in Norway.

In appearance the prawn is a most enticing bait, but it is curious to what extent its attractiveness varies in different rivers, and in divers stages and conditions of the water; and, moreover, as with other baits, it is only a certain proportion of fish in a pool that will take it; and, lastly, with most patterns of tackle there is the uncertainty of securely hooking a "taking" fish.

In some rivers I have found the prawn to be well-nigh useless, in others fish will only take it in dead low water; and, again, in others I have taken fish with it immediately after a flood, when the water has been as thick as the proverbial pea-soup.

I cannot say if the prawn be a good killer in a fly water, as I have not tried it under such conditions.

There are at least three methods of fishing with the prawn: (1) using it as the bait when harling; (2) casting it from the Nottingham reel; and (3) letting it down from a position above the lie of the fish.

Harling with the prawn is a very simple process, and it is scarcely possible for the most inveterate hater of prawn-fishing to take exception to its use in this department, and the only point to be observed is the careful leading of the cast.

In casting the prawn from the Nottingham reel, a certain delicacy is requisite in handling the rod to avoid injury to the bait, which is naturally fragile; and I find

Prawn fishing for Salmon.

it advisable to allow the reel to gently pay out a little line while the bait swings round in the water, so that the prawn is always dropping down stream instead of being held up against it.

Letting the prawn down to a fish is the most interesting phase of this class of angling; in fact, to my mind, it is prawn-fishing proper, and should be effected with great care and delicacy.

I find a spinning-rod, with Nottingham reel and light silk line, dressed with stearine (as described in "By Hook and by Crook"), the best tackle for this purpose. The angler, from bank or boat, should let the bait at an even pace down to the fish; and I find the best way to do this is to remove the check from the reel, and to allow the line to run off between the forefinger and thumb, while the forefinger of the other hand applies to the reel whatever friction may be required.

When a fish touches or takes the bait under these conditions, it is best not to strike or check the line until he has sailed away with a yard or two, for until he has done so, it is most difficult to determine if he have it between his jaws, and occasionally a fish will mess a prawn about before he actually seizes it; but when he carries off a yard or two of line it may be assumed that he has the bait between his jaws, and is carrying it down to his lair, and then is the time to strike. When a fish runs off with

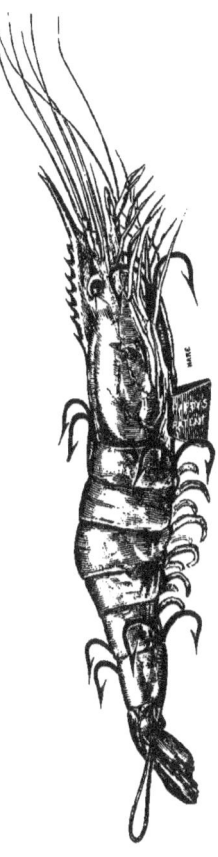

the prawn in this manner, it is long odds on the angler landing him, if he have good tackle.

I have fished with various tackles, from which it appeared impossible for a fish to steal the bait, but they have beaten me over and over again; and it is extraordinary how a fish can nip a portion out of a prawn while keeping his nose clear of the hooks.

They will strip off the head or the tail, or sometimes nip a bit from the back of the head, as cleanly as if it were done with a pair of pincers, and it is therefore essential that these favourite points of attack should be safely guarded by hooks.

It was after considerable experiment and attention to the subject that I perfected the form of tackle here illustrated, and requested Messrs. Hardy Bros., of Alnwick, to make it, in order

Prawn-fishing for Salmon. 141

to meet my and others' requirements, and I am glad to say that it has given general satisfaction. I have killed twenty-seven fish consecutively (without a miss) with this tackle, which is good enough for me.

The tackle looks rather formidable and large, but, when dressed with a prawn, it is surprising how little of it shows; it has accounted for fish up to 68 lbs. in Norway, and many large specimens in British rivers.

The small piece of lead underneath keeps the prawn swimming on an even keel, and almost obliges the fish to attack it in the manner contemplated in the arrangement of the hooks. The tackle is made in two sizes, and the flying triangles are knotted so that either can be cut away without injury to the remainder, *but it should be used entire*. The prawn is threaded with the needle, and secured with silk ties, or small rubber rings, behind the head and at root of tail, and so treated will stand a deal of knocking about. Messrs. Hardy also supply treble and single gut traces, and leads of my patterns, which serve for all methods of prawning. I generally mount a few before starting for the day, carrying them in a wide-mouthed bottle, with the gut loops sticking out between bung and edge of neck.

CHAPTER XVI.

TO SPLIT, CURE, AND SMOKE SALMON.

THE fish to be cured, or kippered, should be laid flat in a cool place, until set firm, and then be split open and cleaned so that the flesh alone remains attached to the skin.

There are two methods of splitting open a fish, either from the back, or from the belly. The former is the neater

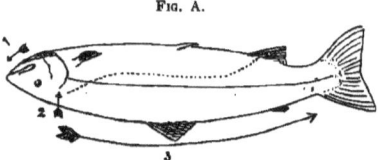

FIG. A.

way for an expert hand, while the latter is easier for a novice; but to make a neat job, a fair amount of practice is requisite for both systems.

To split open a fish from the back, lay it on a table or slab with its back towards you (as in Fig. A), and with a strong, sharp kitchen knife—

1. Split up the lower jaw, lengthwise, from chin to point, as indicated by 1.

2. Make a cut just behind the top corner of the gill-cover straight down from skin to back-bone, as indicated by 2.

3. Run the knife as close as possible along the upper side of the backbone from 2 to root of tail, holding the knife with point slightly inclined downwards, so that the side bones may be severed, as indicated by 3. While

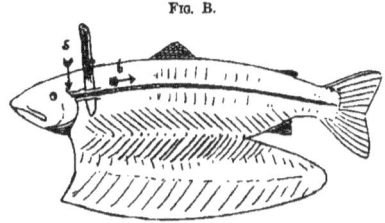

FIG. B.

performing this cut, the point of the knife should follow the course shown by the dotted line in Fig. A, in order to avoid piercing the gall-bladder and the intestines.

4. The top-half of the fish may now be laid back with the hand, and a few touches with the knife should suffice to free the intestines, which are next removed.

5. Make a cut from the under side of the fish, from the skin upwards to the backbone, as indicated by 5 (Fig. B). This, with the corresponding cut 2 in Fig. A, severs the head from the shoulders.

To Split, Cure, and Smoke Salmon. 145

6. Insert the knife behind the gill-cover, and under the backbone, and make a cut from 5 to within a few inches of the root of the tail, taking care to remove as little flesh as possible with the bone, as indicated by 6, in Fig. B.

7. Lift the head and backbone, and snap the latter near the tail, and the flesh remains free of encumbrance.

8. Some smear the flesh with blood from the fish, to impart a red colour at the finish of curing; but whether or no this be done, the fish should now be placed, opened flat, in the saltpan without being washed or dried. Distribute upon the bottom of the salting-trough four double-handfuls of rough salt in crystals (table salt is not so good for the purpose): then lay the fish upon it, skin downwards, and scatter over it four double-handfuls of salt and, if necessary, other fish, with a layer of salt between them, and allow them to so remain for lengths of time in accordance with their individual weights, and the periods over which they are to be preserved.

The following table gives approximately the periods for salting fish :—

Weight of fish.	To keep 1 month.	2 months.	3 months.	4 months.
20 lbs.	36 hours	42 hrs.	48 hrs.	54 hrs.
25 lbs.	40 ,,	46 ,,	54 ,,	60 ,,
30 lbs.	48 ,,	54 ,,	60 ,,	66 ,,
40 lbs.	54 ,,	60 ,,	66 ,,	72 ,,
50 lbs.	58 ,,	64 ,,	70 ,,	76 ,,

Some prefer the addition of saltpetre, or sugar, to the

brine; and, in such case, three tablespoonfuls per fish is sufficient of either, and a few crushed peppercorns may be added.

The fish, upon removal from the brine, should be trussed with three pieces of wood, so as to keep it straightened out for drying, and a loop should be attached at the top, as indicated in Fig. C, by which it should be suspended in a draughty situation *in the shade* until it be dry. When

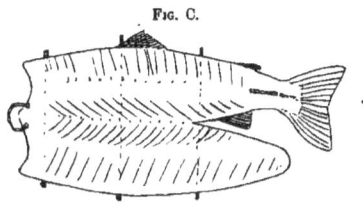

FIG. C.

dry, some lay the fish flat, and pour upon it a glass or two of cognac, and allow it to soak in; but this, like the use of saltpetre or sugar, is a matter of taste. The fish can now be kept in an airy place until required for the table, and, if it be a gaffed fish, it is advisable to plug any rents with a stopping of tow or yarn well soaked in brine, to prevent access to the blow-fly; and it is as well to examine the kippers now and again in case of accidents. Should the fish have to be smoked, it is placed in the smoke-house as soon as dry from the saltpan, and smoked for four-and-twenty hours,

To Split, Cure, and Smoke Salmon. 147

Juniper is the best wood for smoking fish, and perhaps next to it comes oak, or oak sawdust, and care must be taken not to heat the fish in the process; consequently, the fire should be manipulated to produce a maximum of smoke and a minimum of heat.

For travelling, the kippered or smoked fish should be packed in an open crate, or between boards, *not in a case*, and they should be kept in a cool, dry place.

To split a fish from the belly, clean it in the ordinary way for cooking; cut off the head, and cut through the flesh close to one side of the backbone nearly unto the skin of the back.

Now lay the flesh open, and cut out the backbone as above described; then truss out, etc.

A fish of 30 lbs., when salted and dried, weighs about 17 lbs., and after being smoked will, a month hence, have lost another pound.

PART II.

NORWEGIAN SKETCHES.

CHAPTER XVII.

SÜRENDAL.

SÜRENDAL will always be of peculiar interest to me, for in the River Sürna, from which the valley derives its name, I was entered to Norwegian angling.

For the space of five and twenty years previous to my visit to the waters of Norway, my line had been cast in hard places throughout the United Kingdom and the Peninsula, commencing with the leathery-mouthed chub of the Thames; then the trout of Test, Itchen, Thames, Wye, etc.; next the salmon of the Tay, the Galway river, the Blackwater, the Esk, Nith, Annan, Eden, Shannon, and many other streams, lakes, and rivers.

I have no inclination to depreciate the pleasure or value

of angling in the above or any other waters of the United Kingdom, because I am certain that each river or loch, no matter where it may be situated, possesses peculiarities which teaches invaluable lessons to the angler who endeavours to exercise intelligence in the pursuit of sport; yet I fancy many older hands than I am at the game might experience a strange thrill as they should approach a field of operations promising a class of sport superior to that hitherto encountered. By the phrase "superior class of sport," I mean only to imply a greater quantity of free-rising spring fish existing in rapid rivers.

With what satisfaction and anticipation of pleasure does the angler shake off the dust of travel and leisurely unpack his rod-box in some obscure Norwegian valley!

The worries of travel are relegated to the past—the discomforts of steamers are forgotten as the angler quietly settles down for a short term of ease and freedom from the hurry and bustle of the busy world. Human natures are indeed differently constituted. Some folk look forward to an annual sojourn in comparative, or even complete, solitude, surrounded by Nature's handiwork, as the treat of the year; others are only happy when rushing from one point to another—first a voyage by boat, next a railway journey, and a night passed at some foss-side inn, to be succeeded the following day by a drive, a view of a glacier, and so on *ad infinitum*. Well, *chaqu'un à son goût*, and, indeed, fortunate it be that Norway provides opportunities and space for all.

Our foreign neighbours are wont to say that we take our pleasures sadly; but I would rather opine that the tourist takes his pains joyfully, for, in spite of an incessant course of unpacking, and strange quarters, he has ever a smile upon his countenance.

At five o'clock of a fine spring evening, in early June, our vessel heaves-to among the rocky islands which support the wood-built town of Christiansünd.

The buildings, wharf-like, spring from the very water; the town is tranquil, and its people rest idly about the water's edge—for it is Sunday, and all is closed except the Custom House, whither we repair to clear our belongings ere consigning them and ourselves to the little steamboat which will convey us up the inland fjord to the mouth of the Sürna.

Whilst discharging our duties the juvenile natives, with kindly feeling, pluck whisps of fresh green herbage, and place them in the crates which contain our stock of goslings, whose appreciation of the dainty is their benefactor's reward.

As Christiansünd fades to view, we go below to enjoy the excellent repast our host provides—a meal, indeed, excellent of itself, but enhanced by comparison with our food of the few previous days; and barely had we time

CHRISTIANSUND.

to observe the divers and oyster-catchers upon our journey up the fjord ere we lay alongside the little quay of Sürendalsören, the village at the estuary of the Sürna.

We were yet some eight miles from our destination, but as our host stepped upon the quay he was welcomed by his neighbours of Güla, who, with hat in hand, emphasized the pleasure of renewing their acquaintance.

Courtesies were mutually exchanged, and, having distributed ourselves and our *impedimenta* over our host's carrioles and carts, we sped away to his estate in Güla.

We crossed the river by a bridge which had been completed since our host's previous visit, and here, at so late an hour as midnight, the country-folk turned out in full strength to give expression of their thanks for the kind assistance he had rendered towards the erection of the structure.

A curious sight it was for a stranger to witness— many scores of men, women, and children arrayed in Sunday best in daylight at 12 a.m. Amidst mutual salutations and echoing cheers we at length pursued our route, and arrived at Güla about 1 a.m. fully prepared for a night's repose.

The sea-route to Christiansünd, *viâ* Stavanger, Bergen, and Molde, is almost entirely conducted through the smooth water of the fjords, or passages of varying width formed by the mainland and rocky islands which gird the coast.

These stern and, for the most part, sterile piles of granite are characteristic, and in many places grand, notably the peak of Horneln; yet the seaboard after a while becomes monotonous, and the sylvan growth which clothes its inland arms affords welcome relief to the eye.

As we approach the interior, the newly unfolded leaves of the silver-birch, the yellow needles of the pine-shoots, and the fresh verdure of the juniper are in harmony with the emerald green of the fjord-side pastures—indeed, it is springtime, and Nature rejoices that she may discard her snowy weeds.

The ebbing tide borders the fjord-edge with a golden girdle of foliage of the sea, whose fragrance refreshes the mind, as the morning breeze brings health and strength.

Restored by the night's repose, I threw open my casement to welcome the delights of a perfect summer morn—meadows of brilliant herbage serve as foreground to the view, in the middle distance the stately river winds her course, and the yet snow-capped mountains form a fitting background to one of Nature's simple and perfect pictures.

The stern outline, in this rarefied atmosphere, stood out sharp and clean against the clear blue sky, and I hastened to gain the open, unfettered by roof or wall.

Surendal.

I have heard many anglers who have visited Norway for a series of years declare that, regardless of the sport experienced during their visits, it is "the life" they enjoy—and the enjoyment appears to increase in proportion to the number of their annual visits—it is the charm of the country.

The season which I attempt to describe proved to be a late one, and although a few odd fish fell victims to our party early on, it was not before a couple of weeks that a considerable run of fish took place; but time passed pleasantly as we made acquaintance with the neighbourhood and our native companions in sport—while hosts of thrushes, blackbirds, and redwings held evening chorus upon the hillside.

This mountain scenery was entrancing under summer sun and azure sky, but such was not its grandest mood, for as within a few short hours the climate changed, and the lowlands were shrouded in rain-mists, while the snow-wreaths swirled on high, Nature, as a wild beast who knows not restraint, became magnificent in her fiercest temper.

From the commencement of the month of June fine summer weather may not unreasonably be expected, but the elements obey no fixed laws, and, as upon the occasion of my first visit to the country, the weather during the summer months may be wild, cold, and stormy.

For well-nigh six weeks of my stay in Sürendal, cold winds, attended by rain and hail, prevailed, and, in consequence, the river at times was in such state of flood as to prohibit angling, and the temperature necessitated our warmest clothing.

The valley of the Sürna is occupied by a chain of small farms, and saw-mills are situated upon its tributaries, while at a distance of every five or six miles hamlets are established.

My host's dwelling-houses and farm-buildings of themselves constituted a hamlet, and we lived precisely as if in England for the greater part of our visit, as the weather was such as to permit of angling during daytime.

The idea is prevalent that in bright weather it is advisable to delay angling operations until the sun be off the water, and no doubt in many pools this precaution is necessary for sport, but in cold weather I think the day-angler will have the best of the argument, as fish rise badly upon cold evenings, but in seasons when the days are sunny and the nights are warm, the better plan is to leave sufficient undisturbed water for the evening's work.

The lowest beat of the Sürna is of little use for salmon-angling, as fish run straight through it, but it is fairly good for sea-trout, which, however, do not run to any great size upon this river; the largest we killed ran from 2 lbs. to 3 lbs. We fished the beat next above this, a

Sürendal.

stretch of six to seven miles, which is essentially harling water, as, with the exception of a few short casts, the river is of such width, and the fish so few and far between, that by any other method half a day would be required to fish a single pool, and this is more or less the situation in all the big and medium-size rivers of Norway. Above this beat are three others much better adapted for casting the fly, either from boat or bank, but, being further from the sea, the fish, from what I could gather, do not take as freely, and those fishing the beat next above us sorely complained of the necessity in many pools of helping the fly round on account of the slack stream; yet in most seasons more fish would probably be killed in beats Nos. 2 and 3 than in Nos. 1, 4, and 5.

We divided our water into three sections, fishing them in rotation, and working fairly hard whenever there was half a chance. I killed in a period of seven weeks 420 lbs. of salmon, and about 100 lbs. of bull-trout, sea-trout, etc.; and we made the total 660 lbs. of salmon and 150 lbs. of other Salmonidæ.

Two of us were upon our first visit to the river, and our host had not fished it for two or three years, so I imagine, had we been better anglers, and more acquainted with it, we should have made finer practice.

The largest fish we killed was a cock of 30 lbs., which fell to my rod, and on July 23 I killed three fish, 17 lbs.,

15 lbs., and 14 lbs., which was the best day's work for one rod during the season, both for number and total weight.

In no particular of make or shape, excepting some slight local peculiarity, can I detect any difference between the British and Scandinavian salmon.

In previous years fish over 40 lbs. in weight have been taken by rod in this water, but, with the exception of one, which was lost by a member of our party, I think that of 30 lbs. was the heaviest we hooked.

At one time we had on the stone slab outside the house two fish of 28 lbs. each, and a third of 26 lbs., but the smallest was killed the day after the others.

One of these 28-lb. fish was of excellent proportions, and was only excelled in this respect by a hen of 26 lbs., which I killed on June 21, than which I have never seen a prettier. Her length was 42 inches, and her girth 21 inches, and, taking them all round, the fish of the Sürna would lose nothing by comparison with those of other rivers in Europe.

In the month of June we landed two kelts, a cock of 12 lbs. and a hen of 13 lbs., in all probability being about the last to drop down from the uppermost spawning beat, for we saw no others.

This beat, as I have explained above, is but a few miles from the fjord, so it was not surprising that many

Sürendal.

of our fish were ornamented with sea-lice, yet these parasites are not very numerous upon fish which have ascended thirty or more miles of fjord, and I imagine they become detached as the water becomes less salt towards the top of these inland arms of the sea.

The grilse run from 4 lbs. to 6 lbs. and the first we killed upon July 25th, the larger ones being frequently marked by nets. Upon several occasions I witnessed what was to me a novelty, viz. salmon running up in bright sunshine during the midday hours.

They travelled two or three together, at a pace of about two miles an hour, and as they traversed the gravelly shallows, I could trace their movements for a considerable distance.

I also frequently observed fish jumping upon the stream tops after having negotiated the rapid water below, and fish lying in pools would jump with a slight rise of water; otherwise, those settled down rarely showed themselves. At this I was not surprised, for in most rivers of my acquaintance the fish which have been for some days in the pool are those which mostly "put up," but here the fish merely took short rests *en passant*.

Upon July 16, the Sürna was dead low, so to fill up time we went by road and boat to Bœverdal, situated upon the far side of a promontory to the north of Sürendalsören. The river there drains a considerable tract of country, but is nigh worthless for salmon angling, as its gradient is so steep that it quickly runs down, leaving mere trout pools, and to make matters worse the river frequently divides into two or more channels.

Upon our return to Sürendal, the river was dead low, so upon July 19 we set out for Interdalen, which we reached in the evening, after a fifteen-mile drive to the fjord, which we rowed across, then drove about twenty miles, and concluded with a two-mile walk from Nœrdal by a rough footway to our destination, our kit being transported by pack-horse.

Roughly speaking, Interdalen is situated between Sürendal and Sundal, and the approach from the latter direction is far the shorter of the two.

For the last fifteen or twenty miles of our journey a huge pepperbox-shaped mountain of rock had stared us in the face, one of those exasperating beacons which appear to sheer further off the nearer you approach them, as if to show their contempt for the puny means of transport which in their country are at man's command.

At the foot of this rocky hill was situated our destination—an inn, recently built by the proprietor with the assistance of the Norwegian Tourist Club.

At Nœrdal we had been informed that two parties of tourists had preceded us, so we were not surprised to find the inn fully occupied, and ourselves left with the

Sürendal.

choice of retracing our steps to Nœrdal or making the best of a shake-down in a dairy-house.

We decided to avail ourselves of the latter accommodation, and the dairy-maids, who usually occupied the quarters, obligingly cleared out and distributed themselves amongst their friends.

The view from the Tourist Inn is remarkably fine. A little river courses down the fjelds upon the left hand, and partly supplies the two lakes which form the foreground of the picture; the middle distance consists of grassy, undulating slopes, interspersed with masses of broken rock, which lead aloft to mountains of 5000 feet high, including the pepperbox-shaped one I have previously mentioned, upon whose flat summit some enterprising individual has erected a cairn of stones at no little risk, I should imagine, of breaking his neck.

Leading away to the right, and almost facing the inn, a fine glacier takes up the sky-line, and, in obedience to the sun's command, sends forth its substance to dash and foam in countless fosses to add the charm of falling water to the view. The right-hand corner of the picture is supplied by forests of trees and enormous piles of granite, which descend to the lake's margin. Such is the view of Interdalen.

The lake would appear to have been brought into existence by the blocking up of the lower end of this portion of the valley by some terrific break-up and fall of many myriads of tons of rock from the mountains upon either side, and in this manner it suddenly terminates, the overflow making a succession of falls and pools until, several hundred feet below, it subsides into an orderly little river, which, after a course of ten miles or more, descends by a series of fosses, then again becomes a river, and, after a short course, flows into the fjord.

The grand crash which instituted the lake, and filled in some miles of valley with blocks of granite, each many tons in weight, must have been a spectacle worth witnessing—from a distance.

These masses of stone in all shapes and sizes, partly clothed with cushions of growing and decayed mosses, extending from the lake end to the river below were by no means easy to traverse, and being plentifully interspersed with timber, provided sufficient occupation for an angler with rod in hand.

Upon the first morning of our visit we rowed to the lower end of the lake, and by climbing over or creeping under these obstacles, we contrived to reach the first pool, situated 150 feet below the lake, no cool task under a baking sun, with a rod in each hand and a bag on one's back, and as it did not appear to contain many fish, I descended a similar bit of country to the next basin. The water entered, or rather fell,

Sürendal.

into the pool upon the right hand, and flowed across to the left; then, turned by the rock-bound margin, it sped away at a right angle and quitted the pool at the lower end, having traversed three-fourths of its circumference.

I waded out a couple of yards, and seated myself upon a sloping, crested boulder, and, by ramming my heels into a couple of indentations upon the surface, kept myself from sliding into the water six feet below.

I had not left England provided for this class of sport, and had to make the best of a lot of old flies which I found in an almost discarded book. They were mostly quite rotten, but with them I either lost or landed a trout at nearly every cast; in fact, it took me longer to rearrange my tackle than to hook the fish.

I sent the lad who accompanied me to fetch my companion from the pool above, and together we killed 51 trout weighing about 21 lbs. (they being of from $\frac{1}{3}$ lb. to $\frac{3}{4}$ lb. in weight), and after about an hour and a half of this fun, we retraced our steps to the inn. I do not know how many pools of a similar description there may be below, but I should imagine there are a few, judging from the height we were above the little river below.

We killed most of the trout with flies of lake-size, dressed with red body and tinsel rib, with wings of the teal, a pretty good all-round fly for Norwegian trout fishing; but I make no doubt that any other pattern would have served as well.

The lad stood amazed at the pace we killed them, and the people of the inn had never previously seen such execution; indeed, I should not be surprised if the trout had never seen an artificial fly before our visit.

That evening, two rooms at the inn became vacant, so we shifted our quarters from the dairy, and upon the next day set out to fish the stream which fed the uppermost lake.

The innkeeper informed us that the higher we should go up stream the larger we should find the trout, so we walked off in a bee line to strike the river a mile or so up-bank, but as we only landed a few fish of about ¼ lb. weight apiece, we faced about and fished to the mouth with no better result.

Just above where the stream emptied into the lake, a wall of rock rose sheer upon either side to a height of little less than 20 feet; then came a channel about 18 yards wide by 50 long, bounded upon both banks by dense thickets of shrubs growing to the height of a man.

I chanced to see what appeared as a nice quiet rise of a fair-sized trout, and forcing my way through the bushes I cast and killed a nice fish of ¾ lb., and shortly had upon the bank half a dozen of about the same weight. I next moved up to the neck, and cast from the summit of the rocky wall, pulling a few extra yards from the reel while the fly was in the air, and thus managed to kill a good many more, despite the difficulty of landing them, getting altogether 25 trout scaling just upon 15 lbs., all in fair condition, but they would have been better for another fortnight's law.

This was evidently the best ground, for lower down my companion killed but 12 fish of not such good weight, and thus it was clear that the larger fish had drawn up from the lake to feed upon the flies sailing down the river's neck, and, as is generally the case when fish are rising well, the smaller ones kept at a respectful distance.

Thus the innkeeper had laid us on to an entirely false scent, and this little bit of sport, such as it was, we might easily have missed by reason of the bushes shutting out all view of the river.

The next day we returned to Sürendal, having enjoyed a pleasant trip, and I think that the angler who does not object to kill plenty of small fish in exceedingly fine country, might do worse than go to Interdalen.

The river which runs from the base of the rocky

falls to the foss above the fjord is of a milky colour, derived from the glacier-water which feeds it, and upon this account is not worth fishing. We killed in it merely half a dozen trout averaging four to the pound.

We returned to the Stirna in time to avail ourselves of the weekly close time for nets in the fjord, and during the next few days landed several nice fish; then, as the river was low, we planned to visit some lakes eight or more miles away amongst the sæters on the fjelds.

We started off soon after 10 a.m. with attendants and three horses, which conveyed a couple of tents, cooking apparatus, provisions and kit, having previously sent up two boats, for without such few Norwegian lakes can be properly fished.

We were nearly two hours making the ascent of the cliff, which rose sheer within a stone's throw of the house, and after a long, hot march through fine country and hosts of flies, we arrived at the largest lake about 6 p.m., and while the men were engaged in pitching the tents and getting the camp ship-shape, we put off in the boats with the hope of getting a little fresh fish for supper.

The lake was as smooth as glass, yet within an hour or so, we collected seventeen trout of sorts weighing

12 lbs., all but one falling victims to the minnow or spoon; but it was a sultry evening, and the fish rose badly.

With excellent appetites, we returned to find our camp, situated near the brink of the lake, beside a rocky burn, one of many which drained the surrounding fjelds, and charged this natural reservoir with their peat-stained waters.

I have never seen a more deeply-tinted water, for, while bathing, one's legs appeared of the colour of old ale, when but a foot below the surface.

The lake was about 1½ miles long, and varied in width from 200 to 500 yards. The shore-line was irregular, and for the most part deeply fringed with trees and shrubs; similarly ornamented were the many small islands, at irregular intervals, piercing the surface, and affording breeding places for the water-fowl frequenting the lake for that purpose.

The bottom of the basin was composed of slabs of rock and small, tile-like pieces of stone, which in many places around the shore were laid with the regularity of the slater's hand, and at odd places of the bank beds of rushes flourished; but, except at the top narrow end, I observed little growth of weed.

The lake is situated at about the centre of the promontory, which extends to the fjord, between Sürendal

168 Angling Travels in Norway.

and Bœverdal, and is about eight miles from both, overflowing by a small stream which runs into the river draining Bœverdal.

This country is well-wooded, and almost uninhabited, except by the occupants of some sæters in summer time, and shelters a few bears, which generally descend into Sürendal for a little fresh mutton after hibernation.

Seated upon a stone slab, in the drift of the fire's smoke, in the endeavour to keep the mosquitoes at bay, we did justice to a capital repast, and later on retired to our bed tent. Our faces upon the morrow bore evidence of the attentions of the tuneful insects, and after a swim in the lake's tepid water, we proceeded to breakfast, my pal remarking, "Now, if we were in St. Petersburg, we should be selecting our food from fish swimming in a glass-sided tank!" Hinting that if he took his pleasure that way, he could be easily indulged here, I set to work to construct a fish-pond, with the assistance of all hands, from whose finger-tips the skin was speedily removed in lifting the heavy stones. The masonry completed, by directing the rills we so controlled the entire stream, that we could make it course through the interstices of our walls, or could divert any portion of it in the event of a fresh, and for the comfort of its future inmates, we provided shelter from the light and sun by erecting leafy branches around it.

We then put out to fish, and the trout rising fairly well, we soon had thirty or more from ½ lb. to 1 lb. in weight, keeping them alive in canvas buckets during the intervals between our visits to the pond.

In the afternoon we again fished for a while, and by the evening had a stock of fifty upon which to draw at meal-times, thus securing a supply of fresh fish at a moment's notice; and, fortunately, they having mostly been lightly hooked, we only had one fatal case.

It was interesting to watch the fish heading up against stream, while securing the atoms of food which entered the pond.

When we diverted a portion of the stream above, there was a tremendous commotion amongst them as they essayed to escape, thinking, no doubt, there was a possibility of being left high and dry.

As a slight rain set in at evening, we took the precaution to open a sluice above, and when we cleaned our fish for breakfast next morning, we found they contained a deal of food, which the rise of six inches of water had swept down from the ravine.

Within our visit of three days we landed the best part of a hundred trout, by merely fishing at intervals. We saw several ducks and divers with their broods, and a few May-flies, which were rather less in size than the British insect. In the lake we found no less than four species of trout; the brown-trout, the lake-trout, with pink spots and yellow halo, the land-locked sea-trout, and the land-locked bull-trout.

We only killed three lake-trout, the largest scaling $1\frac{1}{4}$ lbs.; of brown-trout and bull-trout there were a few; but the land-locked sea-trout was the principal inhabitant of the lake, and he proved beyond all doubt that the stream formed by the overflow, although now inaccessible, had in previous ages been open for the passage of fish. Many of these fish were short of teeth upon the vomer, but in others the double row was distinct, whereas the three other species had but a single row.

At no time did there appear much feed upon the lake, and in appearance the sea-trout were in worse condition than the others, being of a dusky-brown colour, and elongated in form. But this proved to be a delusion, for, although they had lost class, upon being opened, their flesh was nearly as deep in colour as pink blotting-paper, with curd between the flakes, affording excellent food.

After existing a day or two in the running water of our pond, they became much brighter in colour, but darkened again when killed. Neither of the other three species were worth eating, as their flesh was pale and soft.

Mr. Fleetwood Sandeman, who has visited the lake upon many occasions in previous years, is of opinion that the trout with pink spots and yellow halo, probably the original stationary occupant, had vastly decreased in numbers and size, while the reverse was the case with the land-locked sea-trout.

We found the best fishing-ground to be situated between two islands, about the middle of the lake, where the water was not deep.

One of us killed twenty-five trout while rowing to and fro over this portion, and immediately afterwards another of the party killed ten others in it. We named it the Dogger Bank. The sea-trout were most determined fish, for even when pricked they would follow up the minnow and attack it again and again.

Upon the second day of our visit, the farm people from the valley below brought up their cattle to the sæters around the lake, and as we left, upon the fourth day, they were busy cutting the hay grass. We packed up our traps, and taking it easy over the fjelds, arrived in Sürendal, punctually to take advantage of the weekly close-time for netting in the fjord.

Within the next few days we killed a fish or two and some grilse, but it was evident that nothing much would be done without rain, for the river was spun out.

Upon the last day of our visit, the beginning of August, a rise of a few inches of water gave us a chance of three fish, but not one did we land.

Angling Travels in Norway.

The mergansers, ducks, fieldfares, redwings and redshanks, having launched their progeny upon the world, had left for pastures new. Our time was run out, and so was our tobacco, so upon the morrow we bade adieu to our companions in sport, and as we rowed down the river *en route* to the fjord, each pool recalled to memory the details of success or failure in combat with the salar of Sürendal.

CHAPTER XVIII.

VADSÆTH AND SVARDAL.

AT the commencement of July, Tom and I had almost decided to fish some of the lakes and rivers in the west of Scotland for sea-trout, when we, by mere chance, heard of some water to let in Norway, which, from a somewhat meagre description, promised superior sport with Salmo trutta, and the chance of a few salar.

Upon the following day we interviewed the lessee, and found that we were fellow-members of the Fly-Fisher's Club, which of itself was sufficient introduction, and very little time sufficed to arrange details which gave us the water for the season, and which, from start to finish, proved satisfactory to all parties.

The lessee gave us all the information he had gathered during a couple of days' angling in the locality the previous year, which had resulted in a fish of about 20 lbs., and a few sea-trout of from 3 lbs. to 4 lbs. apiece. This certainly was no brilliant prospect; but we took the fishing with our eyes open, and with the certainty of seeing a new bit of country and water, which I confess have for me considerable charms.

We wrote to advise the natives of our intended visit, and upon July 8, we sailed from Newcastle to Bergen.

Early on the morning of July 10, we arrived in Bergen, and as the boat did not leave for Florö until midday, we spent some hours in purchasing the requisite stores and provisions; for, upon this occasion, we had brought no supplies from England.

From the experiences of this and subsequent years, I find it saves a deal of trouble to obtain supplies in Bergen or Trondhjem, and the only provisions which I take from England are ham or bacon, and lime-juice cordial, which I find wholesome to take now and again where vegetables are scarce, which is generally the case in the country.

If the angler knows his destination some time ahead, it is a good plan to send some seeds of lettuce, etc., by post in advance, so that by the time of his arrival they may be fit to pull, and he can sow a second crop. Green food of this description is a great comfort, especially if the summer be one of continuous heat. We left Bergen at midday, and arrived at Florö shortly before 10 p.m.

We had barely landed our baggage when a boat pulled up to the pier, and one of its occupants, upon ascertaining our identity, informed me that they had rowed down the fjord to take us back.

We had been instructed that from Florö to Eikefjord was a journey of but three hours, so we had intended to proceed at once; but to this the men were not very agreeable, urging that as the tide would be against us all the way, we had better put up in Florö for the night.

Our knowledge of the Norwegian language was at that time extremely limited, and as we had been positively instructed as to the length of the journey, it did not occur to us to put the question to our guides, so calculating that with an hour's rest, and our assistance, if necessary, in rowing, we should make Eikefjord by about 2 a.m., we adhered to our original intention to proceed without loss of time.

We despatched one of the men to procure a few bottles of beer; however, he could only get lemonade, and giving the men a drink of that, and a little of the whisky from a bottle given me at the last moment in Newcastle, we got them into a fairly good humour, and at about 10.30 p.m. started for the head of the fjord.

The night was fine but chilly, and after a while Tom rolled himself up in coats and fell asleep on the top of the baggage, while I took a turn at rowing, chiefly to keep myself awake, for I did not care to leave myself entirely in the hands of strangers, especially, as in this instance, the crew was neither too willing nor expert.

From the start the boat had leaked so fast that one hand had been incessantly at work with a bowl at the stern; but as it transpired that she had been laid up for five months, we thought that the timbers would gradually swell.

Until it became dark at midnight this row up the fjord was enjoyable; then, for an hour before the first dawn of day, the air became rather more dank than was agreeable; but, as it was fairly stiff work to row against the strong ebb, I kept warm and awake.

At 2 a.m. I imagined we should be nearing our destination at the head of this circuitous fjord, and thought I might inquire upon the subject without the exhibition of indecent haste; but I was somewhat surprised when, in reply to my question, the chief of the gang answered, "When we come to yonder mountain we shall be half-way."

The "yonder mountain" appeared to terminate the fjord at a distance of about two miles a-head of us; however, it proved not to do so. When arrived there, I ordered the boat to land for a short rest.

We stretched our legs on the seaweed-covered rocks, and refreshed ourselves with bread and dried herring, washed down with a nip of neat whisky, for there was

Vadsæth and Svardal.

no fresh water at hand, and within a quarter of an hour we were again afloat.

The breaking day, and now warmer atmosphere, cheered us up, and we rowed steadily on until 6 a.m., when the hamlet and church of Eikefjord came into view about five miles distant.

The boat now suddenly commenced to let in water at a pace that no bailing could keep under, and it was evident that the leak must be plugged.

The fjord was at this point more than a mile in width, and the rocky margins so abrupt that landing was impossible; but, by piling up the baggage in the bow, we managed to lift her stern and discovered a hole as big as a snipe's egg, which took some minutes to plug. By the time we got her put to rights a strong and squally wind had sprung up right in our teeth, which completely disconcerted our half-hearted crew, who, upon their own authority, gave up rowing, and hoisted the sail.

The ordinary fjord boat, such as we occupied, has merely two or three inches of keel, and has no pretensions to beat to windward, and the sail is only of use in running before the wind; yet it is difficult to tell how clever a man may be in a boat, so I allowed them to set sail with the almost inevitable consequence that we made a lot of lee-way in a couple of beats.

The men appeared perfectly satisfied with this graceful retreat, and evidently preferred it to forging ahead with the oars; but I was getting tired of the business, and a couple of squalls which were within an ace of consigning ourselves and baggage to the bottom of the fjord determined me to order the sail to be lowered.

The men feigned not to understand, so we ourselves lowered the sheet, and as soon as it was stowed, I ordered three men to row, and myself took the bow oar on the outside, so that I could row the boat's head into shore whenever I desired.

I got her to within a few yards of the shore in comparative shelter, and, determined to give them a good sweating, I kept rowing her head round, so that they were obliged to exert themselves to prevent us running ashore, and thus we travelled about four miles to Eikefjord, and all of us were pretty well done up. But, had I not exercised such tactics, we should probably have drifted about the fjord for many hours.

The church clock struck seven as we ran the boat ashore, and we thus completed a far from agreeable night's work, and were pleased in paying off two of the sulkiest individuals it has been my misfortune to meet.

I am glad to say that neither before nor since have I experienced such unpleasantness with Norwegian

Vadsæth and Svardal. 179

boatmen; but I take it that there exist in all countries all sorts of men, and that what has occurred once may happen again.

As we faced towards the direction by which we had arrived, a delightful fjord-view met our gaze. In this sheltered corner there was merely a ripple upon the water,

EIKEFJORD, 7 A.M.

and although the outline of the hills and mountains which surrounded the fjord stood out sharp and well-defined, the entire scene was mellowed by the early morning haze, which foretells of heat to come, and provides the picture with "feeling" and "atmosphere."

Here was a grand opportunity for the artist's brush, and regretfully I did my best with the camera.

We had been informed that our fishing station was situated at the head of the fjord, and that there we should find our quarters; but here again our information was at fault, for it appeared that an hour or two's tramp over a broken and mountainous country lay yet before us in order to reach Vadsæth Lake, which is connected with Svardal Lake by the river we intended to fish.

We had one man remaining with us, a native of Vadsæth, who was to be our attendant during our visit to the district, and him we despatched in search of conveyances for our kit and supplies. After an hour's absence in the direction of some farm buildings he returned, with two ponies and sleighs, there being no other vehicles in the district, for the simple reason that no carriage with wheels would be of the slightest service over the country we had to traverse.

We secured our traps on the sleighs, and away we went. How the packages survived the journey it is impossible to tell, for they flew about on the sleighs in all directions, and, in the descent of the hill, were as frequently before the ponies as behind them.

After a hot tramp, we arrived close to the border of Vadsæth Lake, and our guide offered to procure us breakfast at his house close by, which offer we gladly accepted, for it was now past 9 a.m., and our previous meal had

Vadsæth and Svardal.

been enjoyed on the fjord steamer at 2 p.m. the previous afternoon.

It was exactly two hours after our arrival that we sat down to a repast of eggs, bread, and coffee, the natives having occupied the interval in running about all over the country-side collecting the food and table requisites. That interval, we both agreed, was not the most pleasant of our existence, but it is best to allow the people to have their own way in these little matters.

An incident, though trifling in itself, was not without humour, especially as we had existed for some hours without a laugh. A good lady having laid the table, and supplied us with food and coffee, was then utterly at a loss to know where to locate herself. First she stationed herself in such proximity to my right elbow that I was unable to lift my arm; not satisfied with this position, she proceeded to pay Tom a similar attention.

We moved not a muscle, nor dared to glance at each other. However, she seemed to think she was not yet in *quite* the right position, so, taking up a chair, with difficulty she managed to squeeze it in between our two, and inserted herself upon it.

The three of us, thus crowded together in about one-fourth the space of the table, would have afforded a touching picture, and we were much relieved in more ways than one when the good lady was enticed away in quest of more coffee, giving us the opportunity to shift our seats further apart.

Our friend, the lessee, at the time of taking the fishing, had arranged for the use of a house at Svardal during his intended visit, and had also agreed to employ our present attendant, whom we will call Johann, at the wage of Kr.2 per day, should he require assistance.

The usual wage of a boatman is about Kr.3 per day in the fashionable rivers of the country, but, further afield, Kr.2½ is about the figure, and in the up-country districts Kr.2 is good pay.

Details, written by a Norwegian of the district, had been handed to us with the lease of the fishing, and when writing from London advising our arrival, we had expressed our intention of carrying out the arrangements, which we naturally concluded would be satisfactory to all parties.

After breakfast, our attendant and temporary host, Johann, endeavoured to persuade us to remain at his house in place of putting up at Svardal, as arranged in our programme.

The accommodation he offered consisted of a room with one small bed, and a sitting-room, both of which were scantily furnished, and had very recently been smeared with inferior green paint.

The family were determined if possible to detain us

(a month's rent is a considerable item in those parts), and, as the last means of persuasion, they declared that they had gone to considerable expense to prepare the quarters at the request of our friend, the lessee.

I felt certain that this was a mere invention of

VADSÆTH LAKE.

Johann's, and we made up our minds, in the first place, to inspect the house at Svardal, so ordered the boat to convey us and our belongings down the lake, telling Johann that if the house did not suit us, we would return to his.

I have, upon many occasions, put up with much

184   Angling Travels in Norway.

worse accommodation, and no doubt we could have managed well enough there, but it did not appear to be a convenient situation for the fishing, and they showed such anxiety to fix us up before giving us an opportunity to see Svardal that we felt sure it was advisable to proceed.

OUTLET OF VADSETH LAKE.

When Johann and his family saw that our plans were fixed, it was clear from their expressions that they thought we should not return, which encouraged the idea that the accommodation at Svardal might be superior.

After a few hours' rest we led the sleighs down to the water-side, and, having stowed the luggage on board,

Vadsæth and Svardal.

we rowed to the lower end of the lake under an azure sky and a baking hot sun.

The lake of Vadsæth is surrounded by mountainous country of rock, clothed now and again with scrub and birch trees. The rock rises sheer from the water-edge, and no road exists until where the Svardal river runs out of the lake, consequently the only means of conveyance is by water.

In less than an hour we ran the boat ashore, at the point where the lake discharges itself into the small river connecting it with Svardal Lake, and, stepping ashore, I walked to the hamlet and interviewed the farmer who owned our future residence, he at the time being busy making hay.

It was at once evident that, to suit his scheme, the crafty Johann had withheld from the farmer all notice of our arrival, and we found the house somewhat in a state of disorder.

As a matter of fact, we paid a good deal too high a rent; but, in passing down the water, I had formed the idea that our stay would be of but short duration, and as we must necessarily put them to a good deal of trouble to prepare the house, I was not very particular about the terms.

At the small hotels and inns up-country, the price for board and lodgings is about Kr.4 per head a day, and for a few weeks together they are glad to take visitors for less.

For a house to accommodate three or four persons, Kr.20 to Kr.25 per week is ample rent, and in private houses, where one lives with the family, Kr.3 per day includes board and lodging.

In the farmhouses up-country they can rarely provide beyond bread, butter, milk, eggs, and coffee, and for these, with attendance, it is the best plan to arrange a daily charge per head—say about Kr.1 in addition to the rent.

The country-folks rarely indulge in meat beyond dried mutton, which they eat uncooked; but it is generally possible to purchase a sheep for Kr.13 to Kr.14, which, however, it may take a day or two to procure from the feeding grounds upon the fjelds. All other provisions must be taken up by the traveller, except in situations where reindeer exist.

I retraced my steps to the boat, and we soon had our kit on a hay-cart and conveyed to our new domicile; then, having arranged for a meal, we unpacked, and got into a change of clothes after our twenty-four hours' journey, preparatory to the evening fishing.

The situation of the hamlet of Svardal is most picturesque; its houses and farm buildings nestle together upon a few acres of rich land, through which the river connecting Vadsæth and Svardal Lake winds its way.

Vadsæth and Svardal.

The banks of the river are well timbered with birch and pine, and the hay-grass and cereals flourish in this humid basin, and are ripened by the intense heat which beats straight down, and is reflected by the rocky walls which almost surround the dale, while the remnant of last winter's snow yet remains upon the mountain summits, as if to bear witness that the sun does not always shine in Svardal.

In fine summer weather it can be very hot in Svardal; for, situated as it were in the bottom of a teacup, the heat cannot easily escape, and is reflected by the rocky walls around.

The crops were both rich and abundant, apparently well-grown in a humid atmosphere and excellent land; and under such circumstances our landlord, who was the largest landowner, was said to be a man of means.

The house was comfortable enough, and, not being encumbered with carpets or curtains, was fairly cool. The furniture included tables, chairs, and beds—or, rather, boxes without lids. The bedrooms were very small, and the beds were unfortunately made of proportions to suit the size of the rooms, instead of the length of the sleeper, and being but about four feet long, it was necessary to roll one's self up into a ball in order to rest upon the moss-stuffed mattresses and pillows which furnished them.

Before starting to fish, I thought it advisable to draw Johann's attention to the clause in the agreement which fixed his pay at Kr.2 per day; and it was well that I did so, for at the mention of this sum he disdainfully tossed up his head and said that the amount was entirely insufficient, adding that an Englishman whom he had

VADSÆTH RIVER.

accompanied when trout-fishing two or three years before had paid him Kr.6 a day.

I surmised that this was an invention prompted by my ready agreement to our landlord's demand for rent; but, as I did not intend to argue about it, I paid him for his services, and told him we should no longer require them.

Vadsæth and Svardal.

At about seven o'clock the sun was off the water, as we set out to fish the river which connects the lakes of Vadsæth and Svardal.

Our original information had been to the effect that the date of our departure would be well suited for the angling season in this district; but Johann had stated, when we met him at Florö, that we were a month too late, and our experiences proved him to be fairly correct.

The stream which connected the two lakes was about 1½ miles in length, and upon the first evening we only killed a lot of trout of from ½ lb. to 2 lbs. apiece, and two or three sea-trout; so we made up our minds that we had no chance of a salmon, as the river was too small then to be the temporary abode of running fish.

The trout in this rapid stream fought well, as also did the sea-trout, which ran from 1 lb. to 3 lbs. apiece, affording good sport with small rods; yet this was not exactly what we sought.

There were many pretty bits of scenery along the river, and, situated at one of the little fosses, was the inevitable salmon-trap, which, during our tenancy, was not working.

Another day we tried our best in Svardal Lake, with a like result; and to all intents and purposes our sport, for the best part of a week, consisted of evening trout-fishing in the river, with an occasional sea-trout.

The morning after our arrival we were surprised to find Johann still in Svardal, and as the night's reflection had induced him to offer his services upon reasonable terms, he accompanied us each day.

HEAD OF VADSÆTH LAKE.

The next day we trolled to the top end of Vadsæth Lake in quest of bigger game, but killed nothing throughout its entire length but trout and a few ill-conditioned bull-trout, and then proceeded to try the small river which ran in at the head, but killed merely trout of smaller size than those in the river below.

The scenery was very fine at this upper end of the

Vadsæth and Svardal.

lake, but the going was excessively bad, as the rocks were steep and their surface extremely slippery; and I found it best to dispense with boots, for in many places a slip would have entailed a ducking.

Johann now proposed that we should try a small river about six miles away in the fjelds, which, he said, con-

SVARDAL FJELDS.

tained trout of a length equal to a pound or so in weight.

We completed a stiff climb under a very hot sun, and found ourselves among the Svardal sæters and a couple of streams which sheltered a lot of small trout, running about four to the pound, and not until then did Johann admit that he had not previously visited the sæters, and that his information had consequently been derived from hearsay alone.

The Norwegian sæter consists of grass-land, and, maybe, an acre or two under cultivation, and upon it is constructed a small dwelling-house of rough make, to shelter the farm hands who repair thither to graze the cattle after the hay and grain harvests have been garnered in the valley.

Each sæter is generally provided with a shed for storing hay, which is either left there, in case of emergency, or, later on, sent down the valley on pack-horses, or lowered by means of a fixed wire.

The sæters are frequently many miles distant from the villages to which they belong, and the milk is sent down daily, or twice or thrice a week, according to circumstances.

Beyond the few provisions we had brought with us, our food consisted of fish, eggs, bread and butter. Of meat there was none, but had we prolonged our stay, we could have procured a sheep from the fjelds. However, we did well enough on this diet, assisted by the bottled beer we had brought from Bergen.

We remained at Svardal rather more than a week; and upon the last night, the farmers asked permission to net the lake, in order to prove that it contained salmon, etc.

Nets were put out over night at three likely angles of

Vadsæth and Svardal. 193

the lake, and upon the following morning, the men brought in two salmon of about 18 lbs. each, and three sea-trout of about 6 lbs. each, all of them being very dark in colour, probably having been up from four to six weeks.

As is frequently the case in rock-bound rivers, the trout here were far from being beauties in appearance, yet for all that were in fair condition; but those found in the gravelly pools, notably the lowest, which flows into Svardal Lake, were as fine in condition and colour as could be desired.

The natives appeared to be all of the same grasping disposition, apparently resolved to obtain as much as possible from strangers upon their first visit, heedless if this policy should result in no future visits to their district. While I was fishing a decrepit old woman, whose rags would have disgraced a scarecrow, approached me and, unsolicited, proposed to bring some multe-berries (cloudberries) on the morrow.

True to her word, she appeared at the lake-side upon the next day, and produced about a pint and a half of berries, half of which were unripe. I took the wild fruit and tendered her 50 ore (6⅜d.), which was beyond their value.

To my surprise, she declared the payment to be insufficient, and held the coin at arm's length towards me.

I recovered the coin, at the same time placing the

2 c

berries on the bank, and shoved my boat from shore; then she altered her mind upon the subject; but, as I neither wanted the fruit or to be bothered about it, I did not grant the privilege usually extended to the fair sex.

While perusing the map and steamer time-table, I, by chance, found a much easier and shorter route between Svardal and Florö than that by which we had arrived, viz. viâ Hopen, a small hamlet situated within an hour's row of the top of the fjord which receives the lake's discharge by means of the little river Osen.

The steamer plied once a week, and, as she was due upon the following day, we decided to take advantage of the opportunity.

Johann had repeatedly solicited a written testimonial as to his abilities, but as we had failed to discover them, we had hitherto adroitly evaded the question; but now, as we intimated our intention to depart, he again urged the request with much importunity.

I wrote out a very fair description of his talents; but, after a night's study of the document, he returned it to me, remarking that it was "not much of a testimonial," in which I quite agreed, at the same time refusing to make any alteration, as I did not think it fair to mislead future visitors to the district. Early the next day, we rowed down Svardal lake, through heavy rain, taking a cart in a second boat, and, when we reached the head of

Vadsæth and Svardal. 197

the Osen river, we transferred our baggage to the wheels, and walked along the road, which for the most part runs in view of the river, until we came to the fjord, a distance of perhaps a mile and a half.

The river was now quite small, and I should imagine that even in a big water there would be little difficulty in casting from bank to bank. The river is let upon lease, and we were informed that upon the first day of that season the lessee had killed ten fish, and seven upon the second day; after that it appeared that little sport had been obtained, and I should class the Osen as one of those small rivers which, except upon very rainy seasons, soon run out.

I make no doubt that at intervals in a wet season a few salmon might be obtained now and again, also a good number of sea-trout, altogether affording sufficient sport to amuse an angler who does not want to fish during every hour of the day, and has other occupations to fill up the spare time; but I should imagine that a man who visits Norway solely for the purpose of angling would, in the majority of seasons, soon tire of the Osen; yet what suits one may not please another, and in what manner a sportsman is to make out his time is best left to the individual.

An hour's row brought us to Hopen, and I had barely time to take a couple of views before the whistle announced the arrival of the fjord boat. Tom proceeded to convey our kit alongside, while I took a picture of the scene, and, in so doing, nearly missed the boat, which would have entailed a week's stay in the pretty but uninteresting Hopen.

We arrived at Florö by 4 p.m., expecting to be obliged to wait at the inn for the Bergen boat, which should leave in the early morning hours. But in this we were most agreeably disappointed, for, within a few minutes of our arrival, the boat en route from Trondhjem to Bergen entered the fjord, being many hours late, and to her we transferred our goods, which, with ourselves and a cargo of salted herrings, were duly landed on the quay at Bergen by 3 o'clock the next morning.

The aroma emitted by the boats which carry salted fish defies description, and the captains say it is impossible to prevent it, for the barrels all leak, and the leakage settling in the bottom of the ship, gives forth an odour which cannot be dispelled by pumping or disinfectants. The cabins and saloons are generally aft, to economize room for cargo, and the consequence is that, when against a head-wind, the perfume aft is more easily imagined than enjoyed.

The decks also are generally covered with barrels and bundles of dried fish, so on deck and below the fragrance is somewhat similar, and can hardly be relished, even by an acquired taste.

CHAPTER XIX.

VOSS AND THE EVANGER RIVER.

IT was towards the end of July that two anglers, depressed in spirits, found themselves stranded in Bergen with nothing to do, and two weeks to do it in—a somewhat melancholy situation.

We proceeded to the Norge Hotel for breakfast, and then made for Mr. Beyer's establishment in the Strandgaden, thinking he would be the most likely to assist us in our dilemma.

At the time I handed my card to one of the assistants, Mr. Beyer and I were strangers to one another, except by name; but, during the brief interval at my disposal, it was evident, by the easy manner in which the staff of both sexes went about their work, that the skipper possessed a mind, officers, and crew competent to tackle the many details of a large and varied business.

The general absence of class distinction, which is one of the characteristics of the Norwegian people, appears in its happiest phase in the relationship between employer and employée. Each appears to recognize that both are doing for the other what neither can perform for himself; there is no obligation upon either side. Much the same feeling exists as between purveyor and purchaser, and I confess that my small requirements are more pleasantly obtained under such conditions than in countries where it is the habit of the seller to cringe and fawn in proportion to the means or titles of his various customers. The Norwegian, from the highest to the lowest in social position, is by nature a gentleman, and is very rarely a snob.

I was appointed spokesman, and discovered Mr. Beyer seated at a desk bristling with correspondence, and, after a few minutes' conversation, we had arranged to take his water upon the Evanger river for a couple of weeks upon his usual terms, which, from the little I knew of it, seemed fair enough.

I do not know why, but hitherto I had certainly been under the impression that my new waterlord's occupation chiefly consisted in the sub-letting of rivers, but the first few minutes spent in his establishment were sufficient to disabuse me of this idea, for it was patent that his tourist agency and general business must render him independent of any small profit in other directions; and my surmise was correct, for he informed me that he was the lessee of

Voss and the Evanger River.

but two rivers, or, rather, portions of the Evanger and the Förde, both small fisheries, upon which any profit that could be made must be small.

In taking a river of a lessee, I should never think of asking him the rent he pays, for I consider that no business of mine; I take or leave it, and, if the former, there but remains for me to pay the rent, and fish it or not, as I may determine, and when my tenancy has expired, the contract is completed. Upon the present occasion, however, Mr. Beyer volunteered the information, which was accidentally corroborated during my tenancy, that the rent he asks is identical with that he pays for the water, plus a small sum which covers the amount of expenditure necessary to provide boats and maintain them in repair; he, however, reserves a few days at the commencement of the season, and all the Sundays, to himself, thus taking out in angling a profit of about ten or twelve per cent., according to my calculations, and, as he remarked to me, I do not consider that excessive, considering the trouble and risk in obtaining tenants.

As a general rule, in Norway the Sunday commences at 6 p.m. on Saturday, and ends at 6 p.m. on Sunday, during which period it is not the custom to fish; but in this district the observance of the Sabbath is not kept by the natives as regards angling.

The Evanger river is about eight miles long, and is the uppermost portion of a waterway, consisting of rivers, small lakes, and fjords, which emanates from Vossevangen lake, and, after a course of about eighteen miles, runs into a fjord proper, a short distance north of Bergen. The Evanger river thus runs out of Vossevangen lake, and it terminates at Evanger village.

VOSSEVANGEN LAKE.

It is a most convenient river for British anglers, for by steamer from England to Bergen, and thence by four hours' rail, it can be reached within forty-eight hours from either Newcastle or Hull. There is an hotel at Evanger, which is rather over a mile below our last

Voss and the Evanger River.

pool, and there is also an hotel at Bülken, the next railway station, situated within a few minutes' walk of

LILAND'S HOTEL, BÜLKEN.

the topmost pool. The latter hostelry stands at a considerable elevation, at the lower end of Vossevangen lake, of which it commands a fine view in the direction of Vossevangen, a distance of about seven miles by road, rail, or water.

The watershed of the Evanger is composed of mountainous and fjeld country, lying in a most exposed position, and is usually visited by more than the average snowfall during winter and the early spring months, as compared with other parts of the country; and, in consequence, there is generally a good supply to maintain the river in angling trim for several weeks from about the middle of June.

It entirely depends upon the weather during June and July how long the stock of snow will hold out, but I may say that, from about the end of the third week of July until the end of the season, the ascent of fish is regulated by the rainfall.

I have fished in a season when the stock of winter snow upon the hills was so great as to have lasted for the best part of two months, with intermittent spells of hot and cool weather; but this pleasant prospect was entirely upset by the rays of a baking sun, which flooded the river for four weeks, and then left it so low, that there could be no rise of water without rain.

Upon another occasion I commenced fishing the river when the snow had departed, and there was no chance of sport without rain; but, fortunately, rain

Voss and the Evanger River. 205

came, and we did fairly well; in fact, in Norway as elsewhere, there is no accounting for the vagaries of weather.

THE VOSS NATIONAL COSTUME.

The contributions from the watershed fall into the lake, becoming clarified in their passage, and issue forth into the river as clear as crystal even when in flood.

At the present time the Evanger river is, by different tenancies, divided into four portions, the first and third being those I have fished. The second and fourth I only know by having walked down them; but, by the method the tenants employ in fishing them, I should imagine they are essentially harling waters, and yield a fair number of fish, which are chiefly obtained in the lower water during the early part of the season.

I have now cleared the way to deal with the first and third portions. The upper water for the first quarter of a mile of its course is merely a useless rapid, unfishable except in very low water, but a fish or two have been killed in it; below this ravine the railway crosses the stream, and the river at once widens out into a large pool a couple of hundred yards long, ornamented by foliage upon both banks. The stream enters the pool with such force that for a considerable distance the water swirls and surges in such queer fashion as to render it impossible for fish and angler alike; but, later on, it subsides into orderly behaviour, and runs from deep to shallow, affording comfortable resting places for fish, and terminates in a swiftly-running head, a favourite resort for those who have ascended the rough water below and the fair-sized foss beyond it.

A SALMON-TRAP.

Voss and the Evanger River. 209

This foss extends from bank to bank, and in it, upon the left-hand side, is a salmon-trap, which, however, from what I know, does not exact heavy toll, and its victims are not the property of Mr. Beyer.

Immediately below the foss an island divides the stream, the left-hand branch being that by which the running fish ascend; then the streams again combine to make one long, wide pool, which stretches out into a wide, lake-like expanse, in which, however, fish are occasionally killed upon the stream side of an island situated in its midst. After about half a mile the lake-water is contracted, and a pool is formed which nearly always contains fish, and lower down, between high banks, is another deep, straight pool, ending in a formidable pass and rapid. This was our upper water, and, with the exception of a few short casts, either from boat or bank on the top pool, is entirely harling water—and, in my opinion, harling water of the most uninteresting description—for the stream is sluggish, and in many places the boat must be rowed at right angles to it in order to prevent the bait grounding. Yet I am told that several fish have been killed in it with the fly in a single day, but this was late in the season after rain.

I take little interest in fishing the water, and for that reason may not have done it justice, and I know it is a favourite abode for big fish, as my companions

210   Angling Travels in Norway.

lost three in it, all between forty and fifty pounds'
weight.

From this water a charming view meets the angler's
gaze in whichever direction he may turn. In the lake-like

THE FOSS.

expanse there are many char, running to about half a
pound apiece.

We walk by beat No. 2 in the other tenancy, and,
entering by a gate, we gain the end of the first pool
of our lower water, and here we find our boatman ready
to row us up to the top of the pool, a distance of 150
yards, or perhaps more.

At a certain stage of the water a small portion can

Voss and the Evanger River.

be fished by wading from the bank; but practically it is a harling pool, although the lays of the fish are so well known in all heights of water that it can be well cast from the boat if the angler so desires; yet, for all that, I consider harling the best method of fishing it.

I have used the word "harling," but, although this is the method I employ in fishing this pool, it does not to my mind correctly describe it, for there is a vast difference between fishing an expanse of water, where fish lie here, there, and everywhere, and fishing such a pool as this where, to the initiated, the position of fish is closely defined at various stages of the water. I harl this pool because, by this means, the fly or bait is so presented best to the fish, and not in order to cover a wide piece of water with economy of time and labour.

The fly is better presented by harling in this and such-like pools, because the water is of such depth and strength that it would be almost impossible to bring it within range of the fish even by casting a very long line.

Below this pool (which generally harbours big fish early in the season) comes a short one, and then a length of swift broken water, which is not of much good; but I have killed several fish in it.

Then comes a pool to be cast from the bank, and in a lowish water it is a pretty good draw.

Below this is more broken water, and then an island divides the river into two streams. The fish pass up by the right-hand corner, and now and again one is killed in it.

Now, two hundred .yards of broken water gradually subside into about one hundred yards of fast-running stream. This, to my mind, is the best and most sporting pool upon the two waters, and I reproduce an article upon it which I contributed to *Beyer's Weekly News* :—

"SALMON ANGLING.

"THE SAGHOUG POOL, EVANGER RIVER.

" About midway between the stations of Evanger and Bülken, upon the Vossevangen Railway, the passenger, if he be not too much absorbed in the study of 'Beyer's Norse and English Words and Phrases,' will observe that the river is spanned by a light suspension bridge, which would appear to have been erected at this particular spot in order that certain death might be the fate of any being who, by accident or design, should fall overboard, for surely not even the best of swimmers could live through that boulder-bestrewn rapid. In contrast to this torrent, the river for the space of nigh upon one hundred yards above the bridge runs smoothly along with but

slightly ruffled surface, although an observer from the bridge would not fail to notice that the gradient is sharp and steep. This is the 'Saghoug' Pool.

"Even if there were no rapid below, it would be almost unnatural for a salmon not to rest here awhile, as it were at some comfortable riverside inn, but the fatigue and labour in ascending the torrent render repose doubly welcome, with the consequence that during the angling season the half-way house is always tenanted.

"The occupants of this pool, however, acquire peculiar habits during their term of residence, the most annoying of which is that if they touch or miss the fly they rarely come a second time.

"Upon the right-hand side of the pool, a stage has been erected to facilitate casting, but in a big water it is best to cast first of all from land above the structure, in case fish should lie high up in the stream, and, under such circumstances, the stage is an inconvenience, if nothing more.

"One day I was so casting above the stage. The fly swung round, and was just about hanging plumb, when about two feet of solid back, crowned with a dorsal fin, pierced the surface, and raised a pretty swirl. Instinctively I struck hard, and found the fly as fast as if it had been in the middle of a hayrick. My 20-ft. Castleconnell is a fairly overpowering weapon, and makes short work of small fry of 20 lbs. or so, but here was evidently a foe worthy of its steel.

THE STAGE AT SAGHOUG.

"My gut and fly were both tried friends, so doubling up the rod I gave it him hot for a quarter of an hour, while he amused himself in exploring the middle and top portions of the pool, until, getting weary, he adopted the tactics always to be dreaded here, *i.e.* making down stream for the rapid.

"I was now standing at the extreme end of the platform, with fifty yards of line out and a big fish pulling his hardest at the end of it, assisted by a heavy stream.

"It was a case of 'pull, devil; pull, baker,' and as I was speculating which portion of my tackle would give way first, to my delight the fish gave a bit, and hauling hard, step by step, I regained the top of the platform, and reeled the fish up to close quarters. It was impossible to net the fish (I am using a net this year in place of a gaff) from the stage, so I again took to the land above, and got him a good way up, when, to my disgust, down he ran, giving me all to do over again.

"Three times I held him with all my strength at that rapid neck, and got him fairly spun out, then hauled him up by sheer force to the top of the stage, and by getting into the water over my knees contrived to bring him alongside a sloping, grassy bank where the landing-net claimed him for its own.

"He was indeed a fine cock fish in prime condition, and scaled 36 lbs., and took three-quarters of an hour to kill.

"The dry boarding of the stage and the weight of the

fish made it hard to keep from slipping, and although I have fished salmon for five and twenty years, this is the only fish who has got me real warm and just a bit done at the finish. The next time you give me a fish, Oh! Saghoug, kindly order him a trifle smaller."

An angler visiting this pool for the first time might think it one of the easiest in the world to fish, and it is as far as concerns the casting. It is true there are some trees near behind from where one casts when the water is big, and lower down the hay-racks (fences upon which hay is dried) stand high upon the rising bank behind, and they have unnecessarily long uprights. I have seen several casts and flies broken in them, but principally through bad casting or right-hand fishing, for if the pool be cast left-handed, as it should be, *i.e.* with the left hand uppermost, there is no reason why the obstacles should interfere, and the angler must merely place his fly *lightly* on the water with a *perfectly straight* line; in fact, he should make an ordinary cast until he arrives at the end of the platform, when a very long and good cast will occasionally give a fish. A few casts can also be made from the bank below the platform, but only small fish lie there, close in; and although, as far as one's chance *there* is concerned, it would be preferable to fish it before casting from the platform, I usually

Voss and the Evanger River. 219

take it last, not caring to run the risk of disturbing the pool for the chance of a little fish of 12 lbs. to 14 lbs.

After the cast is made comes the chief difficulty, for the line must be kept *perfectly tight* in the stream until it comes round to the bank-edge. If this be not

SAGHOUG POOL.

done the fish come up, and, although you may strike the instant you see a swirl or a dorsal ray, he has let go, and you are much too late. It is always worth while to watch a man fish this pool, as you either see sport or fish behave as above. I have seen men miss several fish within a few minutes all on account of slack line, although at the time they did not so account for it, for turning round to me they have said, "Well, I couldn't have been quicker than that," the truth of the matter being that, fishing as they were, they could by no possibility be quick on to the fish, and in reality they did not strike very quickly, for I had seen the fish taking for the best part of a second before they struck.

This may seem rather close work, but it is essential for success in this pool. I made a rare mess of it before I became well acquainted with its requirements, but, acting as I have attempted to describe, the angler should seldom miss his fish.

Fish sometimes may be seen rising within a cast of the left-hand side of the pool, about half-way down; also at the top, off a high gravel bank above; but I have come to the conclusion that these are running fish, for I have rarely seen them in any but a flood water, and, although I have made it a business to fish both these casts every day, I have never even had a touch, and I think the pool from the left-hand bank facing down-stream is practically worthless for angling purposes.

At the foot of the pool there are a few yards of rough water, which break into a rapid nearly half a mile long, and until this year a fish once in it was lost, as there is a light suspension bridge crossing the river, which made it impossible to follow down the bank, but during last

Voss and the Evanger River.

winter a path has been made, and the angler can now follow his fish.

As in most pools ending in a rapid, the fish, when hooked here, usually try to go down at some stage of the fight, and to prevent this the angler has two courses open, either to never allow him to run from the very start, or to let him run on the chance of his hesitating (which they usually do), before going down the rapid, and then to haul him up by main force, or with slight tension to "kid" him up a bit before taking him hard by the head.

I have killed them all ways, and am uncertain which is the best, but at the commencement of the season, with treble-gut, I generally hold them hard, and never give a foot of line. In this manner I killed with single-gut* a fish of 24 lbs. in seven minutes, and another of 18 lbs. in three minutes, counting from the time of hooking until they were on the bank; and so thoroughly killed were they by this severe treatment that, when alongside, they were quiet as logs; but I doubt if one could do this with a rod much less powerful than a 20-ft. Castleconnell.

I am not in the habit of taking the time upon hooking a fish, as I attach no importance to the timing system,

* Cast of two yards treble and one yard single gut supplied by F. M. Walbran at 4s. per cast.

but in these two instances I had consulted my watch previous to fishing the pool, because I made it a rule not to commence before a certain time, and both these fish were hooked within the first four casts.

Below this pool come two bits of bankside casting, one upon either side, and these often give a fish or two. They are formed by stonework thrown out into the stream, affording resting water for fish, and since my first season on the river, Mr. Beyer, at my suggestion and at considerable cost, has constructed many more attractive halting-places.

Next comes a fine, big pool lying between two streams, into which the river is divided, and this always holds fish when the water is in order—very large ones at the beginning of the season. Upon the right-hand side a heavy stream runs against the stone wall built to preserve the road, and just beyond this stream—or, I might say, rapid—is a small cast which generally holds a fish in a big water. It is a long and very difficult cast from the road, as the rapid at the angler's side of the pool so soon sweeps away the fly—so quickly, indeed, that it is almost a fluke if one hooks a fish. I have seen several rises at the fly, but in every instance has he missed it, although upon a single occasion I did not miss him, for, striking very quickly, I foul-hooked him just under the jaw, although I did not know it at the time.

Voss and the Evanger River. 223

I had a terrible time with this fish—over a hundred yards of line out, up to my middle in water, and passing the rod round trees, but I killed him half a mile lower down. He weighed 23 lbs. Since then I always fish

TWO HOURS' SPORT IN SAGHOUG.

this little bit in the boat from the other side, as I consider nothing but a succession of flukes gave me the fish.

This little cast is but the prelude to fishing the pool proper, for the stream upon the left-hand side of the river is that which forms the resting-place of most fish after ascending the rapid water below. Situated between these two streams is a deep pool of horse-shoe form running over a clean gravel bed, and the left-hand side of this shelter is much frequented by large fish for the first few weeks of the season, and by smaller ones later on.

This pool can be fished by casting from the boat or by harling, and the angler is certain to enjoy some fine sport in it.

It is a difficult pool to manage a boat in, and the angler should keep upon close terms with his fish, or he may get broken in the rocks further down.

We have now arrived at the last pool, which is not a good one, and I do not trouble it when there is a chance elsewhere; but, all the same, we have killed fish in it each season by harling.

Below here the waters are in other tenancies, including the Bolstad river. I believe the fishing is all harling, and while passing by I have never seen any other system employed. Then comes a lot of fjord water, succeeded by a river-like portion, which, before its junction with the fjord proper, is trapped and netted in every conceivable way, and the fish are said to run straight through it.

I went down one day, and only saw a seal diligently fishing the best pool, but the farmers get a good number of fish out of it.

Voss and the Evanger River. 225

With fair usage the Evanger should keep up a good head of salmon, for it is water eminently suited to their requirements, and there are fine breeding places both in the river and in Vossevangen Lake, while, in addition to this, it shelters few vermin in the shape of bull-trout and trout, so much so that if your hook touches anything it is long odds on it being a salmon.

The big fish mostly run up in the heavy waters of the earlier part of the season, and grand sport they give.

I have had magnificent struggles with them, and it is best to be pretty smart all round when thus meeting them upon their favourite battle-ground. What a fine sight is a fresh-run springer of 30 lbs. or more when, securely hooked, he jumps clear of rapid water to the height of several feet, sending the spray flying in all directions as he falls, and, to one's delight, the line again tightens!

I have known more than twenty big fish to have been lost by breakages in this water alone during the first month of the season, and this sets one thinking how often a 30-lb. to 40-lb. fish may have been hooked and lost during his career. I fancy many of them have considerable experience in breaking tackle, judging from the very artful devices they employ seriatim in their attempts for freedom.

In fishing the Evanger for the first two or three weeks of the season I think the best plan is to treat every fish you hook as a big one until you see him, and you probably will not be far out in your calculations.

They are apt to deceive you as to their size for some time, as many of these big ones do not exert themselves until you think *your* time has arrived, then they go off as fresh as kittens, and get the first run of you. This very often means a hundred yards' rush and a dive amongst rocks, followed by a breakage, unless you are alert and have a rod and tackle of sufficient strength to hold their heads up. Dee and Usk tackle is of no use here, as a friend of mine ascertained to his cost.

The Evanger fish, in anything like a good water, are very free takers, but if they touch the fly, or even miss it, they rarely come a second time; and it is always necessary to study the light, or glare, upon each pool, for the water is clear as crystal.

The valley of the Evanger is narrow, and the approaches to the river banks are generally abrupt and void of weeds and reeds, so few water fowl frequent it in the breeding season. I have now and again observed a few widgeon race overhead, and for several successive nights I watched an osprey visit one of the lake-like portions, but beyond that I have only seen the usual small waterside-frequenting

Voss and the Evanger River. 227

birds, and, all things considered, I would just as soon be without them upon a salmon river, for, although it is amusing to watch their movements while resting, I can well dispense with them while fishing, for I am weak enough to allow them to distract my attention from the more serious business in hand.

RIVER AT HEAD OF VOSS-EVANGEN LAKE.

I bear no malice against the waterhen, which nearly makes me jump out of my few senses as she scuttles out of the bank-side of a British river within a few yards of my feet, as I wade some pool which fishes best without an artificial ripple, for I suppose I should have made sufficient noise to have afforded her advice of my approach, nor do I bear a grudge against the rowdy fieldfare, for, in pointing out the situation of her nest, she takes me into confidence; but for the merganser, the redshank, and the sandpiper I have not the same regard, for they always seem to imagine that the sole aim and purpose of my existence is to harm them and theirs!

I imagine that during the nesting season they mistake me for the ornithologist in quest of "clutches," either for collection, sale, or exchange, for they take endless pains and waste a deal of time to entice me from their nests or young.

To my mind the most aggravating of these is the little sandpiper, who, as I stroll from pool to pool, entirely unmindful of her existence, thinks it necessary to run and flutter in my path with one wing half outspread and drooping towards the ground.

I suppose she classes me with egg-lifters and four-footed vermin, but I would prefer her to know I am fully aware that if she were suffering from an injured pinion she would probably be lying low in the scrub and not parading her infirmity before my very eyes. What annoys me most in her performance is that, when she considers that I have been misled sufficiently far from her domicile, she suddenly forgets the part she has been playing, and flies back sound in wind and limb, as if to show me how good an actress upon occasion she can be.

I met one sensible sandpiper in my life, who took my measure correctly at the first glance. She evidently decided I was no ornithologist, and took no further notice of me, simply going about her own business. While there were but two eggs in the nest, after my second approach, she would remain looking me straight in the face, and behaved in the same manner until the complement of eggs were hatched out. Her nest was situated in a thin bush about four feet from the ground, unusually high according to my experience. The following spring I looked out for my little friend, but the winter's wear had destroyed the lodging of her old home, and I saw her not.

The white wagtail is also a silly bird, for when she hops up from that crevice among the granite blocks which holds her nest she remains still for a few seconds, and preens herself. She is clever to stand still for a while, for, if in search of her eggs, the very last place I should hunt would be the chink near her, but in preening herself she tells a tale, and distinctly gives herself away.

In certain years there are a great quantity of lemings all along the river-side, and I have frequently seen them swim across the pools at dusk. They are plucky little beasts when cornered, as if you put forward the butt end

230   Angling Travels in Norway.

of your rod they will squat upon their hind quarters and attempt to bite it. I have been told that bull-trout have

FOSS AT VOSSEVANGEN.

been taken with lemings inside them, but I cannot vouch for this. The leming does not make an annual appearance all over the country, but crops up now and again in different parts at an interval of every few years. It is said that they permit no obstacle to divert them in their line of march, and that, rather than be turned aside by fjord or sea, they take to the water and court a watery grave. This is rather a romantic theory, and I know not if it be correct.

Any one looking at the third beat of the Evanger river would probably say it were an easy river to fish, and so it is, but it is astonishing how many fish are lost in it; and, putting aside the fact of their size and the roughness of the streams and river bed, I think this is chiefly the result of letting them get too far away when it is easy to follow them up on land or in the boat. The farmer, who takes the post of gillie in this beat, was at first most averse to drop down to the fish, and, in consequence, I lost many more than I liked. He seemed to think, when a fish showed an inclination to descend into an awkward place, that we could best thwart his intention by keeping from fifty to seventy yards above him; but, in time, I managed to disabuse him of this idea, and we have since had little to complain of, and he now manages a boat uncommonly well, and knows every inch of the water. When, at the commencement of the season, one loses a fish it does not appear of much importance, for there are many other opportunities in store, but losses may easily tottle up to an alarming total in the course of a few weeks, and how one regrets those accidents or blunders when small waters suggest the season's close !

To best fish this river I think the angler should use as big and powerful a rod as he can comfortably wield—a reel with strong check (mine has double the resistance of those in general use, and was made specially for me by Hardy Bros., of Alnwick), to hold 150 yards of line, of suitable weight for the rod. At the beginning of the season he will require the best treble-gut casts and traces, and the single-gut he uses later on should be of the best and strongest quality.

He should be provided with flies of sizes from 7/0 to 3/0, spoons of from $1\frac{1}{2}$ inches to $2\frac{1}{2}$ inches, and phantoms of from 3 inches to $4\frac{1}{2}$ inches, the brown soleskin pattern being as good, if not better, than any others for this water. All other tackle he may leave at home. Upon the first beat I am told that in low water fish have been killed with prawn, but I speak not from experience.

About fifteen miles from Bülken Station, the little river Dale rises, and, after a course of a few miles, falls into the fjord. This river is rented by a party of Norwegian sportsmen, who were kind enough to entertain me with the best of rural hospitality.

The river is small, but contains salmon up to 20 lbs., and many sea-trout, for which it is in reality more suitable ;

Voss and the Evanger River.

but, as one of these friends said to me, "Salmon seem to be like men—some like big houses, others like small." And I thought there was much truth in the remark.

This river has the reputation of having sheltered a fair number of fish in past years, and the woollen-mills erected later are credited with having much reduced their numbers. To make matters worse, the stream at the mouth has split up into two divisions, thus curtailing the opportunities for fish to enter.

The lessees are devising a scheme to re-unite the streams, and filters have been constructed to receive the mill-wash, so they hope that with time the stock of fish will increase. I trust and think it will do so.

Here is an instance of the perseverance of the salmon in ascending a multiplicity of steep pools, each providing a resting place of merely a few cubic feet; and here, as elsewhere, it would appear that Salmo salar will ascend to great heights when he knows, as in this case, that the supply of aërated water throughout winter will be sufficient to provide him with a home.

To give some idea of what sport may be obtained in the Evanger—Two rods fished beats Nos. 1 and 3 for the first five weeks in a recent season, when the conditions were such that few fish were in the upper water—at all events, we only saw one. These rods either fished the lower water (portion No. 3) upon alternate days, or both fished daily by cutting it into two short beats. One rod killed 400 lbs. of salmon and 20 lbs. of grilse; the other rod killed 72 lbs. of salmon and 24 lbs. of grilse; and the rods fishing on the Sundays killed 87 lbs. of salmon—altogether 559 lbs., and 44 lbs. of grilse.

By breakages, or by the hook getting free, the 400-lb. rod lost four good fish; by similar accidents the 72-lb. rod lost sixteen fish—two very large ones; and the 87-lb. rod lost a few; so, with better luck, or more skill, the total could have been much improved.

For the last five weeks of the season two other rods killed just on 200 lbs. of salmon, thus bringing the total to 779 lbs. of salmon, and 44 lbs. of grilse; in all, 823 lbs., principally killed in the lower beat and in a bad season.

The man to whom I sublet the fishing for the latter half of the season I have never met, the arrangements having been conducted by correspondence; but, for all that, I know by his letters that he is a thorough good sportsman. At my request he wrote to tell me how they were getting on, and concluded by saying, "If we had been good anglers, and had possessed any previous knowledge of Norwegian rivers in general, and of the Evanger in particular, I am sure we should have done much better." This is the class of angler I wish to meet, and the kind of man I like to fish with.

Voss and the Evanger River. 235

All that an angler can hope for is that a fish will take the lure ; and, if he do so, all further responsibility rests with the rod-holder. He alone is answerable for the handling, the tackle, and the gaffing, or netting. It is no excuse to say that a fish did so and so ; that the tackle should not have given way, or that the gaffer should have done, or should not have done, something else ; for the rod-holder is, or ought to be, the commander-in-chief, and should mistake occur, he ought to accept the blame—on account of inefficiency upon his part, of ignorance or carelessness in the selection of tackle, or for not having sufficiently instructed his attendant.

This may appear a severe doctrine, but it is one that I apply to myself ; and the longer I fish the more correct does it seem, for seldom is it when I cannot blame myself for mismanagement of a fish lost.

CHAPTER XX.

NORDLAND.

CRUISING about at the close of July I found myself in Bergen, for the purpose of taking the boat for Trondhjem on the morrow, *en route* for Bodø, to fish the Salten river, by arrangement with a friend who had not yet visited Saltdalen.

I was glad to find that a new restaurant had been opened in Bergen, for I am sure that any competition which may tend to improve the food and living in Bergen, and throughout western Norway, should be encouraged, as in the towns the hotels are mostly bad as regards sanitary arrangements, while as to provisions, the meat is of most inferior quality, and beyond a distance of a few miles from the coast, the only fish one gets is the everlasting "lax," and vegetables they scarcely take the trouble to grow.

The country-folk are ignorant to a degree as to the

Nordland.

management of the kitchen garden, and are perfectly content so long as they have plenty of grease (*smör*) of any sort to eat, which, with the exclusion of all fresh air from their dwellings, provides them with their delightfully oily complexions, and fosters sickness in their midst.

The idiotic raptures in which tourists indulge who visit the country but for a week or two have imbued the krone-scenting Norsk country-hotel-keeper with the notion that he has merely to stand by and receive toll for the privilege of viewing his native fosses, fjelds, and fjords, and give as little as possible in return for five or more krone a day.

In many places where the blood of the British coinage has been but once tasted, the natives are grasping and extortionate to a degree, and will not scruple to demand double the correct remuneration.

The proprietors of small inns are pleasant enough, so long as no question arises which affects their pockets; but, should a mistake occur, which is invariably in their favour —for instance, a bottle of wine or a few bottles of beer— then the highly-extolled Norsk will fight for a krone or two as does a lioness for her cubs.

The question of *penge* is apt to expose the weak points of the lower-class provincial Norsk, and, unless one is prepared to be fleeced, this wastes a deal of one's time.

I make no doubt the provincial Norsk is all very well in his way, and, in the aggregate, neither better nor worse than most Europeans, but I fail to see the necessity of lauding him to the skies.

The "steam-yacht" system is putting him in a terrible fright, for it severely threatens to destroy the tourist harvest, as its votaries spend little or no money in travelling inland or at hotels, and "mine host" professes inability to understand why preference is shown for the system.

I have taken pains to make them understand that their inferior food and stuffy hotels, combined with the extortion practised when possible by many with whom the tourist is brought into contact, have created the yachting trips, and that they have only themselves to thank; while as regards angling visitors to the country, their native greed for netting in the fjords and rivers is fast ruining sport, and, as British anglers are tiring of getting a few fish for big rents, the result will follow that Norway will cease to derive benefit from British sportsmen and tourists, and her people will revert to the ignorance and impecuniosity which are so peculiarly their own.

In a country which, to a great extent, is comprised of sea-coast, it is only natural that the fishing population should be in a large majority, and a proof of this is to be found in the repeal of the law passed three years ago, providing an additional day of close-time per week for netting salmon, etc., in the fjords and rivers, yet this law

Nordland.

was repealed by the same Parliament which passed the measure, showing that in Norway, as in other countries, it is possible that the welfare of an industry may be subservient to the requirements of party politics.

At eleven o'clock on a Thursday night I bade adieu to a party of English and Norwegian friends, and left Bergen by the *Nordstjernen, en route* for Trondhjem.

I had early in the day engaged a double cabin for myself and an old friend, who should join the boat at Moldöen upon the morrow, but I was consigned to a berth in a cabin for four persons, for no particular reason that I could discover; but the ways of Damphshib people are peculiar, and I have long since ceased to reason with sea-people of any nationality.

At ten o'clock on Friday morning we lay off Moldöen, and I observed a large boat making from the shore, and in it stood, in the midst of a pile of gun- and rod-cases, a tall individual in an enormous straw hat, holding in one hand a pair of long boots, and in the other a setter by his cord.

My friend, "the old hand," as I usually call him, stepped noiselessly on board in his Lœrdal shoes, and greeted me with the remark, "Well, I didn't know you were going to take me to the North Pole to fish!"

The arrangement for our meeting had been made some months previously when fishing together in England, and we thus met without much discussion upon the subject beyond that contained in a few lines by post. However, we soon fell to comparing notes as to the sport we had experienced during the previous portion of the season upon our several rivers, and discovered that we both had suffered from the same complaint, *viz.* that for a month or more we had been flooded out by the effect of the continued hot sun upon the vast quantity of snow bequeathed by the previous winter.

We soon settled down, consoling ourselves with the idea that at any rate we were about to see a new bit of country, whatever the sport might be.

In the early morning we put in at Christiansünd for an hour or so, and then proceeded on our way to Trondhjem. About midway between these two sea-ports we had to pull up on account of a heated bearing, and during the delay the purser hailed a small fishing-boat, and purchased eight röd fish of about two or three pounds apiece for a krone the lot.

The fish had been caught by hand-line, and upon asking the men why the eyes of some of the fish were projecting half an inch from the head, and covered with a glass-like film, they said that such fish had been captured in water of 100 fathoms or more deep, and that this was invariably the case under similar circumstances.

We arrived at Trondhjem at 5 p.m. on Saturday,

and having placed our baggage on board the steamer *Vesteraalen*, to leave on the morrow, we adjourned to the Hôtel d'Angleterre, and passed the hour before "*aftens*" in purchasing a few stores at Kjelsberg's, the local provision dealer and grocer, who speaks English and provides all ordinary requisites.

The Hôtel d'Angleterre is a fairly good house, but "the old hand," who, by-the-by, has sixteen years' experience of the country, took exception to the charge of Kr.1.40 in our bill for lights, a distinctly modern charge.

The old capital, Trondhjem, compares favourably with Bergen in design and cleanliness. The streets are laid out on the parallel and right-angle system, and are very wide, to prevent a general flare-up in the event of fire. The town must have gained in importance since the construction of the railway, as my friend states that at the time of his first visit grass was growing in the streets.

At eight o'clock the following morning, Sunday, we left for Bodø by the particularly neat and clean little steamboat, the *Vesteraalen*, and met as fellow-passengers an Englishman and his wife, who were proceeding to shoot rype (willow grouse), with the assistance of a team of spaniels, and estimated their bag at 2000 brace. They had rented the shooting for some years, and paid their annual visit after fishing a river near Trondhjem, which

242 Angling Travels in Norway.

they incidentally stated yielded about 1000 lbs. in an average year. The rocky hills and mountains rising from the fjords in the neighbourhood of Troudhjem are mostly round in form, and give the sterile coast an undulating appearance; but this entirely changes as Bodø is approached, for a series of clustering mountains cleave the sky with their peaks and crags, which in shape resemble the teeth of a saw, and the entire coast assumes a sterner

SALTEN FJORD.

aspect; in fact, Nordland differs greatly from more southern Norway. I suppose either the Glacial Period or the Gulf Stream is the reason—they are held accountable for many such peculiarities.

We arrived at Bodø at 1 p.m. Monday, and were surprised to find so many vessels in the roads; but, in addition to the large fishing fleet, it appears that all

Nordland. 243

steamers plying between north and south touch at Bodø. Thus with steamers, fishing-smacks, and a multitude of small craft, the town is a fairly busy place, and looked both lively and picturesque as the bright sun played upon it and the rugged mountain heights with which the anchorage is surrounded.

Our delay was short in Bodø, but upon the return journey I was detained there unavoidably for thirty hours, and from various sources obtained much information respecting the fishing industry carried on there, and in the neighbouring Lofoten Islands.

The Grand Hotel is so but in name; however, it is now being rebuilt, and the proprietor is very civil, and speaks English.

Bodø is a very cold place in winter, as a deal of snow falls, and it is swept by cold winds, which pile drifts halfway up the houses; and I understand this is the case with most of the coast towns and villages in Nordland.

A LADY OF LOFOTEN.

There is a very old church a few miles out of Bodø, and a fine view, extending to the Lofoten Islands, can be obtained by ascending a hill within about two miles of the town. Both are well worth a visit.

Bodø is the business centre of an enormous trade in fish, chiefly herring and cod, which are sent to England, Germany, Spain, Portugal, and Italy; the herrings being salted and packed in barrels, and the codfish are dried. This trade brings a large number of merchants and travellers to the town, and the requirements of the population of fishermen have, of course, to be supplied.

In Nordland during the winter months little more than five hours of daylight is enjoyed, but the Northern Lights are of such brilliance that by them it is even possible to read.

The herring fishery should commence about the first of July, but this year they are very late in putting in their appearance, and they were not expected, under those circumstances, to arrive before September, the consequence being that the men and boats have been idle for a couple of months. The best and fattest fish will only keep a few months when salted, but those of inferior quality will last a year.

I learnt that the small herrings realize from Kr.2 to Kr.8 per barrel early in the season, but later on the fish of good size and quality sell from Kr.10 to Kr.16 per barrel, and that at any price under Kr.2 per barrel they do not pay for the getting, and such are mostly disposed of to an English guano manufacturing company near Bodø.

The herring fishing lasts pretty well all through the

winter until the cod fishing commences in the Lofotens in February, and continues for about two to three months.

During this period about 25,000 to 30,000 men and from 5000 to 6000 boats are employed in the fishery, which are controlled by many local laws. For instance, they are not allowed to fish when they like, but a bell rings as the signal for the boats to put off; then splash they all go into the water in one unbroken line, as if they were starting for a race.

The boats used for this fishing are of the Nordland pattern, and are of such shape that when capsized by accident they will float bottom upwards and enable their late occupants to sit upon them.

The tackle used for cod fishing is as follows:—A long line is floated at regular intervals and buoyed at each extremity, and from this line are suspended a number of other lines of about from four to five fathoms in length, and each of these lines is armed with a weighted double hook.

The fishermen fill their boats, and continue to fish until they have caught so many more as, when tied together, they can tow to land.

In the summer and autumn months a large quantity of coal-fish is also caught in this district. This fish is good food when fresh, but is mostly dried and forwarded to foreign markets, and, as it is of inferior quality, finds its way chiefly to Italy, where, apparently, they appreciate a cheap article.

At various small fishing stations between Bodø and Trondhjem we collected large numbers of herrings packed in barrels, but these were mostly fish of inferior quality which had remained in the fjords since the previous

A NORSK "HERRING-SMACK."

season, and consequently were much inferior to those coming straight from feeding in the open sea.

Upon our arrival at Bodø we at once transferred our baggage to the fjord steamer, which should sail in the afternoon for Rognan, at the head of the Salten Fjord, and then called upon Mr. Jentoft, the British Vice-Consul, and agent for all the steamers, who kindly sent one of his assistants to aid us in the purchase of a few provisions.

My "old hand" considers he is wise in the matter of food, so I left the catering to him. He purchased at Walkimton's shop coffee, sugar, and a few other necessaries, not forgetting a case of the native ϙl, and then proceeded to other shops to procure meat, bread, etc. I entered the butcher's shop, and found him triumphant at having successfully negotiated for a lump of the hock part of a leg of beef. I ventured to inquire if he intended to purchase soup-meat, and was immediately suppressed with the reply, "You don't want to buy bone, do you?" I guessed that the subject was more tender than the meat, so said no more. He said he was sure we should get nothing in the valley, so laid in a stock of cheese, butter, etc.; in fact, with the exception of the ϙl and beef, he carefully selected such articles which we could have procured of much better quality up-country. However, he knew not that at the time.

Most people I have met have little fads about food. I must confess to a weakness for marmalade, and my "old hand" cannot exist without cayenne pepper and onions, so we purchased a supply of each and ordered the lot to be sent on board the fjord boat, and repaired to the Grand Hotel for *middag*.

248   Angling Travels in Norway.

Upon an expedition such as this it is scarcely fair to dictate to one's partner as to his choice of provisions, but I believe that upon future occasions I should feel it but consistent with a sense of duty to emphatically bar onions, for the simple reason that a single knife is used to prepare all articles for the pot, and the consequence is that the same flavour will be apparent in all your food, not that I am unduly prejudiced against the succulent bulb, but I think it possible, *now and again*, to dispense with its attractions.

After a good *middag* we repaired to the fjord boat and paid the boatman for bringing the pet provisions on board, and away we sailed at 3 p.m. on Monday for what we understood at the time to be a journey of six hours to Rognan, but here our calculations were much at fault, for although the distance direct is only about seventy miles, the boat crosses and re-crosses the fjord so many times for the collection and delivery of the mails, passengers, and goods, that she only arrives at Rognan at 6 a.m. the following morning.

The boat was crowded, and as the atmosphere of the saloon bore the true Norsk flavour, we decided to pass the night in the smoking-saloon, a chamber of about 9 feet by 6 feet.

For many miles the fjord is bordered by prosperous-looking farms, and we learnt that the land was good and

Nordland.

the rainfall usually sufficient. The little creeks were occupied by fishing-smacks waiting for the unpunctual herring, whose appearance was also anticipated by shoals of porpoises which sported in all directions.

At a distance of something less than twenty miles from Bodø the fjord suddenly narrows, and for the length of about half a mile or so is little more than 200 yards in width. Through this narrow channel the forty miles of fjord above is refreshed with every tide, and the entrance and exit of such an enormous volume of water creates an immense whirlpool of half a mile in length; and so great is the force of its currents and surging eddies that vessels are unable to ascend the passage for the space of two hours before and after high tide. I was told that the German Emperor's yacht essayed the feat some two or three years ago, but had to abandon the task, and was fortunate to escape unharmed.

The fjord boat departs from Bodø to suit the tide at the "Saltström," as it is named, consequently passengers by her do not see the whirlpool at its best; but I advise any one having spare time in Bodø to devote half a day to view it at high tide. It is renowned throughout Nordland, and is said to be more powerful than the celebrated whirlpool of the Lofotens; and I have seen nothing which conveys more forcibly

250   Angling Travels in Norway.

to the mind the vast power of water under partial restraint.

For the best part of 100 yards from each side of the fjord the water seethes in countless, ever-shifting whirlpools, which meet in the centre of the passage; but at favourable states of the tide there is a centre

ROGNAN.

course which is comparatively calm upon the surface. Yet the steamer rolls as if upon an Atlantic swell, and her contortions are felt in a peculiar manner by those standing on deck, as with her engines at full speed she does no more than two miles an hour, and it appears difficult to keep her straight.

At five a.m. Tuesday morning the boat stopped, and

Nordland.

upon gaining the deck not a soul was about. Lighters came alongside, and I ascertained we were off. Rognan, and that the navigators of our boat were making the most of a couple of hours' rest.

As from deck I viewed the entrance of Saltdalen at Rognan, the valley appeared to be of about two miles in width, hemmed in upon both sides with birch and pine-clad hills, which reached inland as far as the eye could see. The river ran into the fjord upon the left hand; then came a tall-spired church, and from that point to the right-hand extremity a belt of pine trees is drawn up in line as if to repulse the invader; and these are fronted by rows of substantially built boat-houses, which extend to the strand, and house the nets and tackle of the fishing-boats, which now ride idly in the bay, expecting the arrival of the herring.

Upon conveying our baggage to land the case of provisions was missing, and no key was attached to the bl case, which was rather a severe blow to my "old hand." However, we placed the kit upon carts, and adjourned to what is facetiously described as the Hotel of Rognan, where we procured a very fair breakfast, then wired about the presumably lost case, called upon Herr Norman, the Landsman of the district, and then proceeded by road to Sündby, a distance of about four miles, where we intended to remain a few days to fish the last seven miles of the river.

Arrived at Sŭndby, the Enke Larsen descended from hay gathering upon the hill side, and accorded us lodging in her house, situated within a stone's throw of the river; then we unpacked our kit, and, having arranged for a meal of some sort, we started off to assist the pot with our rods.

The bl case was broken open without much ceremony, and amongst the bottles we discovered the stores which should have been in a separate case; this put rather a different complexion to the *menu* of our *middag*, and restored my "old hand" to his habitual composure.

In a couple of hours we killed a few sea-trout, one of 4 lbs., which immediately fell into the pot; then we dined, and set off to fish what we were told were the best pools of the lower water; but only killed about 25 lbs. of sea-trout, ranging from 2 lbs. to 4 lbs. a piece.

That evening there was a slight rise in the river, and the following day we killed a grilse of 5 lbs., and about 20 lbs. of sea-trout, three or four scaling about 4 lbs. each. Thus in a day and a half our bag merely consisted of one grilse, 5 lbs., sea-trout about 40 lbs., one bull-trout, one brown-trout, and one sea-char of about ¾ lb. Our boatman told us that harling with compound tackle

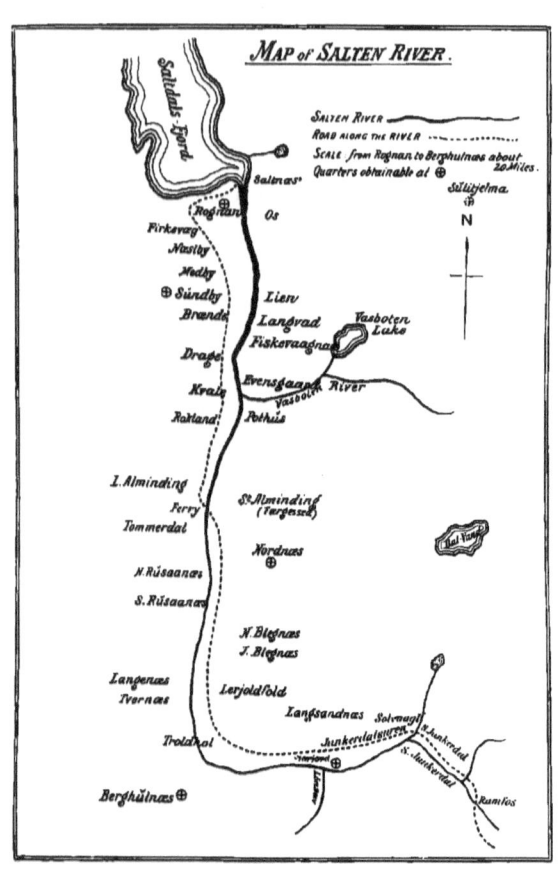

Nordland.

was the best game here; however, we killed these fish mostly by casting the fly.

A day and a half was quite sufficient of this class of sport, and we came to the conclusion that there were no salmon in this lowest beat, and, moreover, that there was little prospect of any without rain, for although the

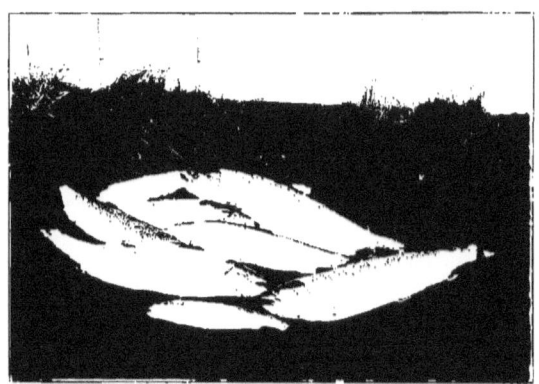

GRILSE, SEA-TROUT, BULL-TROUT, TROUT, AND SEA-CHAR.

river was big enough in all conscience, the natives considered it very low, and that a big rise in the water would be necessary to wean the fish from the attractions of the herrings in the fjord; so we decided to push on early next morning to Storjord, situated at the head of the top beat of the river, and about twenty miles from Sundby. From the fjord to Storjord is about twenty-four miles, and for angling purposes this is divided into three and a half beats, the three lower beats being of about seven miles each, and the Storjord, or top beat, consists of about three and a half miles, with which goes about three or more miles of the Junkerdal river, to which the Salten changes its name at Storjord.

Fashions in ladies' dress even penetrate Saltdalen, for the little *pige* who drove our cart sported a dress of a shade of heliotrope, which I believe was the fashion in England not so long ago, and more remarkable still were the sleeves of her bodice (or blouse, I believe, is now the correct term), which were puffed out from shoulder to elbow in quite the up-to-date pattern. Fashion truly appears to travel faster than most things to Saltdalen.

As we were packing up our traps the inevitable old man of the hamlet turned up and indulged in the usual idiotic remarks, and, what was a greater nuisance, a letter from Landsman Norman to say that the Forstassistent at Storjord regretted his inability to entertain us before Saturday, two days hence, as in the mean while he expected a visit from the Finance Minister of Sweden.

This rather upset our arrangements. However, we decided to proceed to Berghülnæs, four miles short of Storjord, and take our chance of quarters there.

The country does not run to carrioles, so we engaged

two carts to convey ourselves and the baggage we required, leaving the heavy things with Enke Larsen.

The road was rough but sound for about ten miles, but, after fording the river at Alminding, it became little more than a track for a few miles, until at Nordnæs we struck the new road, which eventually is to be extended to the Swedish frontier.

At Alminding there is a ferry establishment, with large and small boats to convey passengers, carrioles, and horses, and I strongly advise travellers to have their kit, etc., taken over in one of these *in all states of the water*, but the horses and carrioles can ford the stream easily when the river is low.

At the time of our visit the river was fordable, and the driver of the foremost cart, through sheer obstinacy, gave the contents of the vehicle a ducking.

Fortunately, the load consisted of cases and packages, which were little harmed, but it was merely a piece of luck that he was not driving the cart which contained clothing, dry plates, and cameras.

Upon such occasions it is unwise to trust to the natives, as they do not quite appreciate to what extent one's kit may suffer from a wetting, as they possess little which would hurt by such treatment.

After crossing the river we drove three or four miles through wooded avenues, and then halted to enjoy a luxurious *middag* of Dutch cheese, rye bread, and øl, while the ponies grazed along the roadside.

From Rusaanes the new road was very loose and heavy, and, as one of our unshod little beasts was getting footsore, we had to tramp it for the remainder of the journey. The country people will not shoe their ponies until the last moment, and not even then, if they can avoid it.

Arrived at Berghülnæs, we found that the hamlet consisted of merely a couple of farms situated across the river. They were invisible to us, but half an hour's shouting and whistling produced a wild-looking individual in a boat, who, however, could not put us up, as his rooms were engaged for travellers expected that night. So, in preference to lodging in a hayshed, we decided to push on to Storjord, where at the worst we were sure to obtain as good quarters.

The farms at Berghülnæs are situated about a mile from the river upon the opposite side to the road, and are approached by a very rough route; indeed, it is merely a track, mostly uphill, leading to a plateau of cultivated land.

From Berghülnæs to Storjord the road runs through forests of birch and pine trees, which clothe the hills upon either side of the river, and snow-crowned Olfjeld, 5500 feet high, serves as a background for every view.

An artist could find material for a picture at every turn of the road, but the landscapes would much resemble one another.

We suddenly turned from the main road into a track through the pine forest, and, with half a mile's jolting, were shot into Storjord, which, like most of the hamlets along this valley, would be difficult of discovery to the uninitiated.

We questioned the only farmer in the place about putting us up for a couple of nights, but as from him we could only extract a meaningless grin, we tried our luck with his old lady, who asked if a single room leading out of the dairy would do for us.

The apartment was redolent with the odour of sour milk; but, as the "old hand" suggested, we could soon smoke that out, and we thanked the old lady for her proffered hospitality ; but, previous to unloading our kit, we thought it advisable to visit the Forstassistent, who, they informed us, lived close at hand.

We were fortunate to find him at home, and more fortunate to find that he could put us up, for the Swedish Minister had unexpectedly changed his route ; so, making matters right with our friends at the farm, we dismissed our carts, paying the men Kr.6 each, that being the charge from Rognan to Storjord, a distance

260 Angling Travels in Norway.

of twenty-four English miles, and we then prepared to settle down.

The only living thing we had seen upon the road, excepting the fieldfare, was a large hawk, named in Norwegian the mouse-hawk.

THE FORSTASSISTENT'S HOUSE.

Our host, Herr C. Nieuwejaar, held the Government appointment of Forstassistent over a large district, for which he had qualified some sixteen years ago by several years' study of forestry in Germany, and lived, with his wife and family, in a comfortable house and farm offices built for him by the Government, and it did not take us long to discover that we were extremely fortunate as regarded our quarters and entertainment.

Nordland.

His house stands within a few yards of the river, a portion of which he has the right to fish, but he only kills very few fish in a season, as his duties take him far afield.

He is a sportsman according to his native lights, and kills rype with his Storjord-made gun, which cost Kr.54 and weighs 11 lb., so at all events he got plenty of metal for his money. The weapon, like his fishing-tackle, is of peculiar make and shape.

He speaks English, French, and German, which is a good deal more than we could do with a combined effort, and is no mean performer on the piano and flute; in fact, he is just the man one would have expected not to meet at Storjord. I am exceedingly obliged to him for much information concerning the district, and for his general kindness and courtesy.

Saltdalen derives its name from some salt mines, which formerly existed near the fjord, from which it extends (including Junkerdal) to the Swedish frontier, a distance near upon fifty miles, but from Storjord to the nearest point of the frontier is only about fifteen miles.

The climate of Nordland throughout autumn and winter is colder and more severe than that of more southern Norway, and at Storjord for months together during winter they experience from 20 to 33 degrees Fahrenheit of frost, with a metre of snow in the valleys; but there is no wind, or the place would be uninhabitable.

As in all northern districts, here travelling is easier in winter than in summer, for upon long, wooden runners (ski) a man can reel off the twenty-four miles to Rognan within four hours. There is also considerable sleigh traffic during winter, and, amongst other commodities, large quantities of coffee are imported from the nearest Swedish town, more than 150 miles distant, which pays no duty, as the Government apparently does not consider it worth while to incur the enormous cost of maintaining Custom House officers along its lengthy frontier.

Of goats there are plenty, but the climate at the head of the valley is too rigorous to encourage sheep-breeding, although lower down the valley they are bred and can be purchased of the farmers at about Kr.13 a head.

About Junkerdal wild raspberries, currants, and many other small berries beloved by birds grow in profusion, and the multebœr is common on the fjelds. Potatoes and peas are cultivated in the gardens, all being ripe by the middle of August.

Throughout summer time the mosquito makes music in the air, showing no distinct preference for the bedroom or the country-side; the cleg alights noiselessly upon your hand, and immediately attends to business, now and again relieved from duty by the angry wasp.

Very few elk have been seen in the neighbourhood within the last dozen years, but bears are more numerous, as from three to five are killed each winter.

Wolves penetrate from Sweden, and do a deal of damage amongst the herds of goats and sheep, but fortunately they are not abundant.

The capercailzie I have seen within a few yards of the house; rype, ptarmigan, black-game, woodcock, and snipe may be found during summer within a few hours' walk of the river, and of course during winter low down in the valley, and the hare is an all-year-round inhabitant, but to the best of my knowledge this valley, and the hills which flank it, afford but indifferent sport for the gun.

Better and, I believe, really first-class rype shooting can be obtained on the borders of Sweden, where at the first frontier station of Merkenæs quarters are obtainable, but it is advisable not to attempt it until a few nights of frost have cut down the mosquitos.

Most of the shooting-ground about Storjord is Government property, and in order to pursue and kill game a licence is requisite from Christiania, otherwise a fine of Kr.200 is likely to be incurred. The Government reward for killing wild animals, etc., is as follows :—For a bear, Kr.40 ; for wolf, Kr.20 ; for fox, Kr.4 ; for eagle, Kr.2 ; but our friend would have the first two bounties reversed, as he considers the wolf does far more damage than the bear. Until the last year a pair of large eagles were in the habit of nesting in the crags above Storjord, but I believe they succumbed to a Lapp hunter.

I saw some Lapps in Bodø, who herd their deer and exist within a few hours' walk of the northern part of Saltdalen, but do not descend into the valley except to purchase provisions and dispose of their meat.

At the present time it is estimated that there are between 1500 and 2000 Lapps in Nordland, but they are rapidly decreasing in numbers, and a few years hence will have died out altogether, or will have retreated to Finmarken.

They live in tents made of canvas, which in winter they pitch upon the snow, and for flooring they use dried branches of silver-birch gathered in summer. They crowd into these tents with their dogs, and thus keep themselves warm, while the aroma of the atmosphere quite defies description.

In summer they are dressed in garments made of blanket or of cotton cloth, and in winter the reindeer provides them with raiment.

Their food consists of reindeer meat and cheese made

from the deer's milk, but the milk itself they do not drink, neither do they eat bread, vegetables, or salt, except a little of the last commodity in their coffee, which is practically their only beverage while upon the fjelds and mountains.

Their dogs are perfectly trained to herd the deer, and as the women-folk do all the small work, the male Lapp does scarcely anything beyond the market business and hunting and trapping the wild inhabitants of his district, either to dispose of as food or for their skins and the Government rewards.

In the summer they breakfast at leisure, then repair to the nearest glacier or snow-mountain, upon which they recline during the heat of the day, thus taking advantage of the cool atmosphere, free from the flies, which infest the fjelds.

Upon their visits to the valleys for supplies, and to sell their meat, they always endeavour to obtain brandy and tobacco. The production of the cognac bottle is the prelude to all transactions, and the Lapp prefers to beg rather than to buy.

The meat of a tame deer weighs from 50 lbs. to 60 lbs. Eng., and is worth from Kr.25 to Kr.30.

The Lapps hunt the bear, the wolf, the brown and the black fox (the skin of the latter being most valuable), and they trap the smaller game.

Of recent years a Lapp has been known to kill in the neighbourhood of Storjord five bears and many wolves in a season. The bears are captured in the springtime, and the wolves they hunt when the snow is deep and soft, for in this the beast sinks, while the Lapp on his long wooden runners (ski) runs him down and kills him with a stick.

Knowing the Forstassistent to be a Government official, the Lapps frequently request him to address his chiefs on their behalf upon many subjects, and during their visits in winter, in common humanity, he is obliged to give them shelter in some outhouse against the intense cold of night.

Lapp names are not uncommon in the district—for instance, the Viskis, the name of a tributary of the Lons river, a tributary of the Salten; and about the valley one occasionally meets with specimens of humanity whose appearances testify to a cross between Norsk and Lapp blood.

In the vicinity of this valley the natives apply themselves assiduously to the capture of rype, etc., when they are easiest to get—viz. in the winter, for then the birds descend into the valleys for food and shelter, and, by reason of the temperature, they can be safely despatched to foreign markets.

The favourite method to trap the rype is by building a

long wall of timber and branches, in which small passages are constructed at intervals, each being fitted with a snare upon the draw-noose principle, and the black-game they secure in a more wholesale fashion, for these birds flock together and bury themselves under the snow, leaving a vent for air at the top, over which the sporting native spreads a net and scares the birds into it.

The Forstassistent tells me that in this district there exists a long-standing aversion to the woodcock and snipe as articles of food, and, as he does not share in the general opinion, he gets whatever there may be of this class of shooting pretty much to himself.

As regards sport upon the Salten and Junkerdal rivers, we killed very little beyond sea-trout, although there were two spates of a couple of feet apiece during our stay, yet perhaps I may venture to describe the rivers from an angling point of view.

Within a short space of time it is always a matter of considerable difficulty in any country to ascertain the sport a river affords in an average year, as the country people do not value sport by the same standard as does the angler, and it is also frequently to their interests to imagine that the fish in a river are both larger and more numerous than they would appear to be to one unprejudiced.

In Norway, or, at all events, in its more unfrequented

parts, this difficulty is somewhat enhanced, as it is often the custom to bestow the term "Lax" (Salmo salar) upon sea-trout.

In nine cases out of ten the distinction between the two species is known, and I think the term "Lax" is applied thus generally for these reasons, that for eating purposes in their homes the two fish are of equal value, and the people are so little educated in the sport of angling that they see no difference in this respect between a 10-lb. salmon and a 10-lb. sea-trout. I am speaking of districts practically beyond the range of markets, and it should be noted that the Norwegians in the country always put fish into the salt-tub, for they so prefer them to fresh fish.

It amounts to this—that the farmers fish, shoot, and trap for the pot alone, except it be for reward; and, inasmuch as your attendant or boatman is often one of this class, the reasons he adduces to account for the absence of fish are frequently more ingenious than correct, his principal object being, in their united interests, to retain the angler as long as possible in the district. I do not mean to say that the above is always the case, for I have met several men who have told me in a straightforward manner the truth about a river, but I have more frequently derived this information after I have discovered it for myself, and, so to say, the game was up.

Nordland. 269

However, from my own knowledge of the river from source to fjord, from what I know has been killed in it for the last four years, from information of what was done in it ten years ago, and from the information I have received as to how the farmers treated it in the interval

JUNKERDAL.

while it was unlet, I think I can give a fair description of it, and the sport it is likely to render for some few years to come.

The Junkerdal and Salten rivers together run a course of near upon twenty-eight miles. The Junkerdal river is in reality a rocky torrent. About three miles above Storjord there is a kind of pool; there are no others in the river, but there are hundreds of little runs in which fish can and no doubt do spawn. I have seen both salmon and sea-trout in them far advanced by August 10, but they will not take fly or minnow.

I merely tried them for experiment, as there is no sport in hooking fish in such places; in fact, I write off the Junkerdal as practically useless for angling purposes, but valuable as a nursery.

The Lons river, which joins the Junkerdal at Storjord, may be dismissed, as it is very shallow, and sea-char alone frequent it.

We have now from Storjord to Rognan to deal with, a distance of about twenty-three miles, and I should reduce this by the distance of about five miles, from near Drage to Rognan, leaving a distance of about eighteen miles for angling.

I write off the five miles between about Drage and Rognan, as there the river is very wide, and the pools, such as they are, being very small, offer little inducement for fish to rest. They are not what I call salmon pools, and are the best portion of a mile apart.

The Salten river from Storjord may be described as a wide, sweeping river, running over a gravel bottom, which is continually shifting, and, roughly speaking, in accordance with my ideas, there frequently is no more than one pool in each three-quarters of a mile.

Nordland. 271

Every now and again, one side or the other of the river is bounded by rock, in such situations are the pools, but the water frequently rushes in with such volume and speed that three-fourths of the pool is in a boil, and only a few yards remain near the bank, or at the tail, where fish can rest.

The Vasboten Lake discharges itself by a small river of the same name into the Salten river at Evansgaard, and in a big water good sport may be had with sea-trout and sea-char in both river and lake. It is scarcely necessary to describe the pools individually, as they are so similar.

The Salten comes down of a milky colour in a flood from the Junkerdal and the washings from its own banks, which form a grey deposit upon the bottom for its entire length.

If I had to fish the river I should bestow my attention chiefly upon the casting-water included between the Bræ Pool, near Drage, and the Berghulnæs Pool, and, to cut it still further down, I should take from the Bræ Pool to Nordnæs, distances respectively of about fifteen miles and eight miles.

At the present time salmon in the Salten, I imagine, are few and far between. The river is far too big for interesting fly-casting, and I take it that harling is the most practical method of fishing it; at all events, I cannot fish vast expanses of almost untenanted water by casting the fly. With a well-stocked river there would be more encouragement so to do.

I calculate that the fish run up in an average year between the middle of June and August 1, and if three rods over the best portion were to kill twenty fish in five weeks, I should say that sport was what they might expect. I should have a boat at each of the pools between Drage and Nordnæs, and walk from one pool to the other, as the labour and expense of carting would be great, and it is a nuisance drifting down useless water.

The gradient of the Salten is steep, and as the bed is composed of gravel, with no small fosses or rocky falls to make pools, the bed is constantly changing.

From reliable information the Salten has not been even a fair salmon river for the last fifteen years, and I very much doubt, if left to its own devices, it ever would become one, at all events not for a number of years; and it would always require to be fished in the manner I have described in order to cover the fish lying scattered all over the water.

The Salten has more the cut of a sea-trout river, and I think that any one laying himself out for this sport would have a good time.

July and August should be the best months for

Nordland.

sea-trout, which run to 6 lbs. or more, and many are of 4 lbs. and 5 lbs. weight; but the large fish run up pretty early, about the middle of July.

Some of these fish run right up to the Junkerdal, but many of them branch off from the main stream, and run through the Vasboten river to spawn in the lake.

I should opine—in fact, I know—that the Salten is a very good river for sea-trout, and should suit those who like to kill fish in a big river with spoon, minnow, and fly; while, when in order, the Vasboten river yields a capital bit of fishing.

There are many sea-char (a fish I have not met with south of Nordland) in the rivers, and good sport may be had with them in Vasboten Lake, in which they take even while the sun shines brightly.

We found the people of the valley mostly obliging, and anxious to assist us in every way, but of fishing they know next to nothing, and the men who rowed the boats harled very badly, and possessed not the slightest knowledge of how a boat should be managed for an angler casting the fly.

As is the case with most rivers, I was told that, *in times gone by*, the Salten was rich in salmon, but, taking it in its present form, it would require a very large stock of fish to make a decent show, and the only plan to accomplish this within ten or more years would be to establish a large hatchery, then I think decent sport might be enjoyed by those whom it pleases to harl a large river; but, by reason of the natural disadvantages which I consider the river to possess, a much larger stock in proportion would have to be annually bred than would be the case in a river more suited by nature to the habits of *Salmo salar*.

Fish ascending a river coloured with grey marl get tinted with it, and I should think it very doubtful if they appreciate the decoration; but in the Salten river this scarcely applies to the sea-trout which ascend the Vasboten river, as it is but a short distance from the fjord, and the fish soon lose the colouring matter in clear water.

I should roughly estimate that two or three good anglers would, in an average season upon the Salten river and its tributaries, kill the best part of 300 lbs. of salmon, and 700 lbs. to 800 lbs. of sea-trout, bull-trout, sea-char, and trout, the bulk of which would be sea-trout. They might easily make a better bag.

During the intervals when the river has been unlet the indiscriminate and greedy netting by the farmers has evidently much reduced the stock of salmon; and if any one should essay the task of restocking the river, he should make the farmers pay heavily for their greed, and take care of himself as regards drawing up a lease.

I descended the river from Storjord to the fjord by a

raft, constructed by the kind orders of the Forstassistent, who did everything in his power to make our visit enjoyable; and I must say he succeeded admirably.

Saying good-bye, and wishing him a speedy realization of his expectations to promotion to an Inspectorship, I stepped on board the raft, which dashed into the first rapid amidst a roar of dynamite, exploded for my benefit on shore.

The raft was constructed of ten pine logs of 22 feet each, lashed to cross-pieces with ropes of twisted birch boughs, and was sufficient to support four persons, a lot of luggage, and three large cases of empties, which served as seats to keep us clear of the water, which continually swept the raft from stem to stern. The logs, having intervals of about two inches between them, allowed the deck to quickly clear itself of water while negotiating the many rapids of the first ten miles. She was steered by an oar at each end, and although the journey, perhaps, might not suit nervous dispositions, she was so steady, even in the rapids, that a glass of liquid placed upon the cases would not have been upset, thanks to the skill of the steersmen.

The native footgear in the valley, except during winter, when they wear fur or reindeer skin, is the Lapp boot. The piece of leather which forms the sole is gathered up all round, and covers the foot, leaving uncovered a tongue-shaped space in the top; into this space a second piece of leather is sewn. The boots reach to about six inches above the ankle, and are folded and secured by a thong which connects two eyelet holes, one upon each side of the instep. In continuation of this thong, or lace, is about a yard and a half of webbing, which is wound round the top of the boot and the trousers, thus serving as a watertight legging. The boots are frequently soled and heeled with two pieces of single leather, and are so much larger than the size of the wearer's feet as will admit of a light all-round lining of fine hay. They are first-class boots, and a dressing composed of oil and tar renders them waterproof, but they are rather slippery footgear, when the fjelds are wet with much rain.

From Bodø to Bergen we touched at thirty different places, and during the earlier portion of the journey those who delight in sunsets had a grand time.

Once a week there is a quick service from Bergen to Hammerfest, which, at the time I write of, sailed from the former port on Thursday nights. The mail and passengers wait a night in Trondhjem, and continue the following morning by the "*Vesteraalen*" steamer, which, being heavily subsidized by the Post Office, carries only passengers, mails, and parcels between Trondhjem and Hammerfest, and *vice versâ*.

Thus from Trondhjem to Hammerfest the traveller can

be free from the odour of the dried or salted fish with which all other boats are loaded, but from Trondhjem southwards he can scarcely escape it.

For the northern portion of the journey there is not much difficulty in obtaining a two-berth cabin to one's self, but from Christiansünd it is another matter, as from there the boats commence to fill up.

Most of the North Cape tourists apparently travel by the yachting steamers, as we only met two British subjects in the boats north of Christiansünd.

From my short experience I certainly prefer Nordland to more southern Norway, but, as I have attempted to explain, it has its drawbacks and inconveniences apart from the length of the journey, which occupies about a week from London to Bodø and a day or so more upon the return journey.

In Nordland the country-folk are glad to furnish one with lodging (which generally means a bedroom and sitting-room), cooking, and bread, etc., for about Kr.1.50 a head per day; or, if they are in a position to do so, will lodge and board one Kr.$2\frac{1}{2}$ to Kr.3 a day, and I dare say it might be done for less, especially for any length of time. The charge for boatmen is Kr.2 to Kr.$2\frac{1}{2}$ per day.

Norwegian food, taking it all round, is of poor quality, and I think I may safely predict a reduction in weight as the result of a couple of months' sojourn in the north country, or, to put it in another way, the food is filling at the price, but it has not much "stay" in it.

Under the kind auspices of the steward, I enjoyed a two-berthed cabin all the way back—or rather, I should say, as far as Molde, where the ship was full up—and by chance there came on board a nice little *Lofotenske pige*, quite the prettiest of her race, whom I had met a few weeks earlier in the season.

The ways of Norwegian ladies are somewhat unconventional *en voyage*, and I have met them travelling in parties and singly without escort, but it is the mode of the country, especially in the north, where every courtesy is extended to them. Upon the occasion of our first meeting I took the *Lofotenske pige* out fishing for a little while upon two or three occasions; she knew not a word of English, but when she hooked a fish she used to amuse me, as, turning round, she would say, " Yay veel, vhat dou say, trag dee sool oot af heem?" And, no mistake, she did.

I should not forget to mention that within a few hours of Bodø there is a new place for tourists, but as yet it is only visited by the Norwegians of Nordland, and, consequently, there would be no annoyance by the objectionable class of British tourist, who seems to be now neglecting his favourite Isle of Man for the fjords.

Sulitjelma is about twelve hours by boat up a fjord

a little north of Bodø, thence up a series of lakes by boat, and then by a short length of railway through particularly fine scenery. There is good accommodation.

The shortest way to get from England to Nordland would be by direct steamer from Newcastle or Hull to Trondhjem, arriving there in time to leave by the "*Vester-aalen*" at eight a.m. Sunday.

In Nordland they make most palatable sweets with all the lowland and fjeld berries, the favourite form being a jelly, but instead of using gelatine or grain they employ a little potato meal, and this is their only dish which appears to me worthy of imitation.

"My old hand," more fortunate than I, prolonged his stay at Storjord, and has informed me that the rype shooting in that immediate neighbourhood was disappointing. So it would appear that it does not become good until the top of the Junkerdal, towards Mercanæs, the first Swedish frontier station.

Herr Landmark, the Inspector of Norwegian Fisheries, has published his latest report, which ends with the year 1890. British anglers are rightly of opinion that the Fishery Inspector has the interest of the Salmonidæ at heart; he, however, takes a more sanguine view of the Salten river than I can do, and reference is made to a salmon hatchery upon its banks, which does not now exist.

There are so many proprietors of fishing rights upon

this river that if each obtains but a small sum in rent, say £1 or so per annum, the total must amount to what, in my opinion, is much beyond its present value as a *salmon* fishery.

Herr Landmark and others interested in the welfare of the salmon fisheries of Norway are anxious that her rivers should be rented by anglers, as thereby the nets are bought off and the number of spawning fish increased, and this is effected, in most instances, at a profit to the riparian proprietors.

A large majority of the rivers are fished by sportsmen of the British Isles; and to the rents paid by them may be chiefly attributed any improvement which may take place in the freshwater fisheries of Norway.

APPENDIX.

AN ABSTRACT OF THE SALMON-FISHERY LAWS OF NORWAY.

The chief provisions of the new Salmon Fisheries Act are as follows :—

1. It is forbidden to fish for salmon or sea-trout in the sea from August 26th to April 14th, or on rivers or lakes from August 26th to April 30th ; but rod fishing is permitted to September 14th—all dates inclusive (§ 1).

2. From September 1st to April 14th, both inclusive, it is illegal to sell, to expose for sale, to buy, or to receive salmon or sea-trout. But this clause does not apply to receiving, by way of present, salmon caught by rod and line not later than the 14th of September (§ 2).

3. From 6 o'clock on Saturday evening till 6 o'clock on Monday evening it is forbidden to use any appliance for catching salmon or sea-trout, or to let any appliance remain in the water so as to catch such fish or to interfere with their free run. But this clause does not apply to fishing with rod and line (§ 3).

4. On the petition of County Councils (the "Amtsformandskab"), the Crown may, by royal ordinance, extend the weekly close time for bag-nets or similar nets on the sea, and for any appliance used for catching salmon or sea-trout on the rivers or lakes, save rod and line (§ 4).

5. Nets for catching salmon or sea-trout must have a width in the mesh of not less than 5·8 centimetres from knot to knot, when wet (§ 5).

6. The interspaces between the bars of fishing-traps must be not less than 5·8 centimetres wide (§ 6).

7. Salmon or sea-trout which may have been caught in nets with smaller meshes than 5·8 centimetres from knot to knot, or by turning off the water, must be returned to the water, unless the length of the fish exceeds, if salmon, 55 centimetres, or, if sea-trout, 40 centimetres ($=15.72$ in.) (§ 8).

8. It is forbidden to place trimmers in such portions of a watercourse as are frequented by salmon (§ 10).

9. It is unlawful to use appliances on such a watercourse as aforesaid which are of such a nature as would catch young fish of less than 21 centimetres (= 8·27 in.) in length (§ 11).

10. It is illegal to place any fixed net or any other fixed engine at a less distance from the midstream-line than $\frac{1}{8}$ of the breadth of the river. And if such nets or engines are placed on opposite sides of the river within a distance, along the course of the river, of 100 metres (= 109·4 yards), it is illegal to place any of them nearer to the midstream-line than $\frac{1}{8}$ of the said breadths (§§ 12–14, cfr. § 19).

11. Within a distance of 100 metres (= 109·4 yards) from any fixed net or other fixed engine with a leader, placed on a river frequented by salmon, it is unlawful to use any drift-net or seine (§ 16, cfr. § 19).

12. When petitioned by County Councils (the "Amtsformandskab"), the Crown is empowered to fix, by royal ordinance, a stretch at the mouth of a river, within which the use of seines, or bag-nets, or hang-nets, or similar nets, is illegal (§ 17).

13. On the petition of County Councils (the "Amtsformandskab"), the Crown is empowered to prohibit or to limit, by royal ordinance, the use of drift-nets on fjords and rivers frequented by salmon (§ 18).

14. On such portions of a river, including lakes, as are frequented by salmon or sea-trout it is unlawful to use leisters, spears or similar appliances for catching fish. It is illegal to use such appliances for catching salmon or sea-trout in the sea (§ 20).

15. It is unlawful to use any explosive or poisonous stuff for catching fish in rivers (§ 22).

16. On the petition of County Councils (the "Amtsformandskab"), the Crown is empowered to grant local dispensations from most of the prohibitive sections of the Act (§ 23).

17. Contraventions of the above-mentioned provisions are punishable by fines from Kr.10 to Kr.500, and the fish caught, or bought, or sold, or exposed for sale, or its value, and, in some instances, the nets or traps used are forfeited (§ 25).

18. The Act further introduces a new and more efficient system for enforcing the provision of the Act (§§ 27–33).

Appendix.

PATTERNS OF SALMON FLIES.

(*A Plate facing Chapter XII.*)

SANDEMAN No. 1.

Tag: Gold thread, purple silk.
Tail: Golden pheasant topping.
Butt: Black ostrich harl.
Body: Jointed in three divisions of equal length of yellow, orange, and red silk; gold tinsel from butt to head.
Hackle: In three joints—yellow, orange, and red.
Shoulder-hackle: Black hackle red at points.
Wings: Mottled brown turkey, grey turkey, golden pheasant tail, dark mallard, four narrow slips blue-dyed swan, two broad slips dun turkey, four fibres peacock harl.

SANDEMAN No. 2.

Tag: Gold tinsel thread and yellow silk.
Tail: Golden pheasant topping.
Butt: Black ostrich harl.
Body: One-third orange floss silk, two-thirds dark blue silk and gold tinsel.
Hackle and shoulder-hackle: Blue-dyed cock's.
Wings: Light mallard, brown mottled turkey, golden pheasant tail, gallina, yellow-dyed swan.
Topping: Golden pheasant.

SANDEMAN No. 3.

Tag: Silver tinsel.
Tail: Yellow floss silk.
Body: Pale blue silk, silver tinsel.
Hackle: Pale blue.
Shoulder-hackle: Reddish brown.
Wings: Light mallard, golden pheasant tail, a few fibres of yellow-dyed swan, two sprigs of golden pheasant rump.

SANDEMAN No. 7.

Tag: Gold tinsel.
Tail: Whisp of orange pig's wool.
Body: Lower half orange pig's wool, upper half brown pig's wool, gold tinsel.
Hackle and shoulder-hackle: Brown.
Wings: Under, dark mallard; upper, brown or dun turkey; whitish at tips.

SANDEMAN No. 11.

Tag: Gold tinsel.
Tail: Yellow floss silk.
Body: Three turns orange pig's wool, remainder black pig's wool, gold tinsel.
Hackle and shoulder-hackle: Light red brown.
Wings: Golden pheasant tail, bustard, grey turkey, white and red-dyed swan, two wide slips of glead hawk, or brown turkey.

INDEX.

A

Angling rights, 46
Angling season, 8, 18, 19

B

Boats, 50-53, 177
Bødo, 236
Bœvedal, 159, 168
Bull-trout, 88-94, 157, 170, 252

C

Char, 99, 100, 210
Christiansünd, 150
Climate, 16-18
Close-time, 30, 31
Clothing, 17, 18
Coal-fish, 245
Country-folk, 46-49, 150, 181, 193, 194, 237, 268, 273
Cure and smoke salmon, to, 143-147

E

Eikefjord, 175, 179
Evanger river, 199-235

F

Fish-passes, 27
Fjelds, 171, 191
Fjords, 28, 31, 32, 36, 150, 154, 176
Forstassistent, 260, 261
Foss, 209

G

Glacier, 98
Government rewards, 264
Grayling, 101
Grilse, 65, 159, 252

H

Harling, 115-126, 138, 211
Hay-racks, 218
Herling, 87, 88
Herring, 244
Hopen, 197
Hotels, 185, 199, 203, 236, 241, 243
Houses, 182, 187

I

Interdalen, 160-165

J

Junkerdalen, 269, 270

K

Kelts, 33, 66, 158

L

Lakes, 14, 39-42, 71, 166-171, 185, 273
Lapps, 264-266, 275, 276
Legislature, 30, 46, 238
Leming, 229, 230

Index.

M
Marking fish, 70, 72-75, 78-82

N
Nets, 28-38
Nordland, 236-280

O
Ova, 63, 72, 90

P
Parr, 64
Pine-logs, 33
Pollution, 233
Prawning, 137-142
Prosecution, 32
Provisions, 174, 186, 192, 236, 241, 247
Pylorics, 66

R
Raft, 275
Reindeer, 265
Rent, house, 185, 277
Renting rivers, 127, 136
Rivers, 8, 21-27, 52, 148, 189, 200, 232, 236, 266, 267, 270
Röd fish, 240
Rype, 263, 279

S
Sæter, 42, 171, 192
Salmon, 10, 57-82, 157-159, 217, 221, 222, 225, 232, 233

Salmon-fishery laws, 30. *See also* Appendix.
Salmonidæ, 24, 25, 27, 28, 31, 54-101
Saltdalen, 236-280
Saltströmen, 250
Sea-anchor, 53
Sea-char, 100, 101, 252
Sea-louse, 68, 159
Sea-trout, 82-88, 157, 170, 252
Sleigh, 180, 184, 262
Smolt, 64-66, 102-105
Snow, 11, 18, 23, 201
Steamers, 150, 198
Sunday, 201
Sürendalen, 148-172
Svardalen, 173-198

T
Tackle, 106-113, 140, 163, 232
Tapeworm, 68
Temperature, 13, 74
Traps, 28-38
Trondhjem, 241
Trout, 95-99, 102-105, 163-165, 169, 180, 193

V
Vadsæth, 173-198
Valleys, 107
Voss, 199-235

W
Wages, 182, 188

Y
Year in Norway, the, 10-15

PRINTED BY WILLIAM CLOWES AND SONS, LIMITED, LONDON AND BECCLES.

www.ingramcontent.com/pod-product-compliance
Lightning Source LLC
Chambersburg PA
CBHW022042230426
43672CB00008B/1041